# ARCHITECTURE
## OF THE 20TH CENTURY

# ARCHITECTURE
## OF THE 20TH CENTURY

MARY HOLLINGSWORTH

NEW YORK
A Bison Book

First published in USA 1988
by Exeter Books
Distributed by Bookthrift
Exeter is a trademark of Bookthrift Marketing, Inc.
Bookthrift is a registered trademark of Bookthrift Marketing
New York, New York



ISBN 0-7917-0184-0

Printed in Hong Kong

**Page 1:** Pelli, Pacific Design Center, Los Angeles, California, 1975-6.

**Page 2:** Portman & Assocs, Bonaventure Hotel, Los Angeles, California, 1974-6.

**Page 4:** Mendelsohn & Chermayeff, De La Warr Pavilion, Bexhill-on-Sea, Kent, 1934.

**TO MY PARENTS**

# CONTENTS

# INTRODUCTION

What is the appeal of the classical tradition? In many ways the history of architecture in the twentieth century can be seen as a debate on the role of classical architecture. Classical architecture can convey many images: moral or extravagant, imperial or republican, intellectual or military. Witness the contradiction inherent in the variety of messages contained in the Capitol, St Peter's, the British Museum, the Arc de Triomphe and the villas of Palladio, which all claim a classical heritage. But too many of its messages were inimical to the modern movement, and its very existence posed a threat to the development of a distinctively new style, which was determined to discard the historicism of the nineteenth century.

The modern movement was determined to be seen to be new and classical forms were decisively rejected by its architects. However, it remained a profound inspiration for the theories of Le Corbusier. Architecture reflects the culture in which it is created and the twentieth century is no exception to this rule. Indeed, twentieth-century architects have deliberately set out to create images that would continue their own ideals of a new industrial society, based on equality and would visually stand apart from the errors of the past. But the new images, like the new society, were not generally understood or accepted. If the modern movement rejected overt references to the classical tradition, a surprising proportion of twentieth-century architecture has consistently retained its allegiance to the past. From neo-Georgian housing estates to Hitler's buildings for his new Berlin, the classical tradition has persisted. Attempts to erase historicism have failed. Recent architecture has revived many of the forms of classical architecture, from the orders to the dome, and with them the ability to communicate specific and varied messages.

Like the Renaissance, twentieth-century architecture has attempted to reevaluate the role of classical architecture in the light of modern society. The classical tradition permeates our systems of government, finance, education and culture. Why not our architectural surroundings?

**Left** Horta, Tassel House, Brussels, Belgium, 1892.

**Below:** Frank Gehry & Assocs, Loyola Law School, Los Angeles, California, 1982.

PACH BRO

# 1/NEW STYLES FOR THE NEW CENTURY

Burnham, Flatiron Building, New York City, 1902. A commercial solution to the problem of a triangular site. Financed by a Colorado gold miner, the building is divided and decorated in a traditional manner, simply rising directly over all of the available space.

The effects of the Industrial Revolution were dramatic. The mechanical inventions of the eighteenth century, which increased the efficiency of power-driven machinery, caused a massive upheaval in economic and social life and led to irreversible changes in our perception of the world.

New replaced old. Agriculture was replaced by industry as the main source of economic wealth. Transportation and communications were transformed by the invention of the steam engine in 1825. Iron and concrete were developed as cheaper alternatives to stone and wood. Machinery replaced the hand as a more efficient manufacturer of goods. People were concentrated in urban rather than rural areas. There was a massive population growth, as economies expanded; the result of a rise in living standards and a fall in mortality rates. The population of London increased from 1,000,000 in 1801 to 6,500,000 in 1901. In New York the increase was even more dramatic, from 33,000 to 3,500,000 over the same period. The appalling conditions of the industrial working classes inspired both reformist and revolutionary theories from Robert Owen to Karl Marx. Attempts to realize these ideals led to the formation of new socialist parties, which openly questioned the ruling establishment. The challenge of the new was expressed in architecture. New building types developed in response to the needs of the new industrial society: factories, commercial offices, exhibition halls, warehouses, bridges, railroad stations and low-cost housing for the industrial worker.

Tradition was threatened and expressed architecturally in the design of railroad stations, whose façades were restricted by the cultural conventions of the establishment. Built of traditional materials and designed to emulate styles of the past, these façades contrasted with the stations behind which had vast iron spans, made possible by exploiting the potential of new materials. Protest against industrial progress found expression in the Arts and Crafts movement, based on the socialist ideas of William Morris, who was horrified at the way in which the machine, and mass production, had replaced man and his handicraft. Ironically, it was Morris' rejection of the eclectic style of the establishment and his emphasis on the simplicity and functionality of vernacular styles that formed the basis of the modern movement in architecture.

The challenge to the old, inherent in the Industrial Revolution, gave rise to a spirit of inquiry around 1900, which openly threatened traditionally accepted certainties in all fields of life. Politically, it led to social and electoral reforms throughout the civilized world and ultimately to the overthrow of the Czarist regime in Russia (1917). Scientifically, it increased man's understanding of the world, allowing him greater control of his environment, with the discovery of the electron and helium (1897), radium (1898), the theory of relativity (1905) and the structure of the atom (1913). Freud's *Psychoanalysis* was published in 1910 and Amundsen reached the South Pole in 1911. There were also major advances in transportation and communication. Marconi's invention of wireless telegraphy (1895) led to the first wireless communication between the United States and Europe (1901). The diesel motor was developed (1898) and the first powered flight was made by the Wright brothers (1903). The discovery of helium led immediately to Zeppelin's first airship (1911).

Traditionally accepted rules and restraints in the arts were challenged during the late nineteenth century, by movements such as Arts and Crafts, Art Nouveau and Impressionism, and were finally abandoned by Picasso

**Below:** Jenney, Fair Store, Chicago, Illinois, 1890-1. The replacement of solid masonry by skeleton-steel frames revolutionized architecture and allowed for the greater height demanded by businessmen.

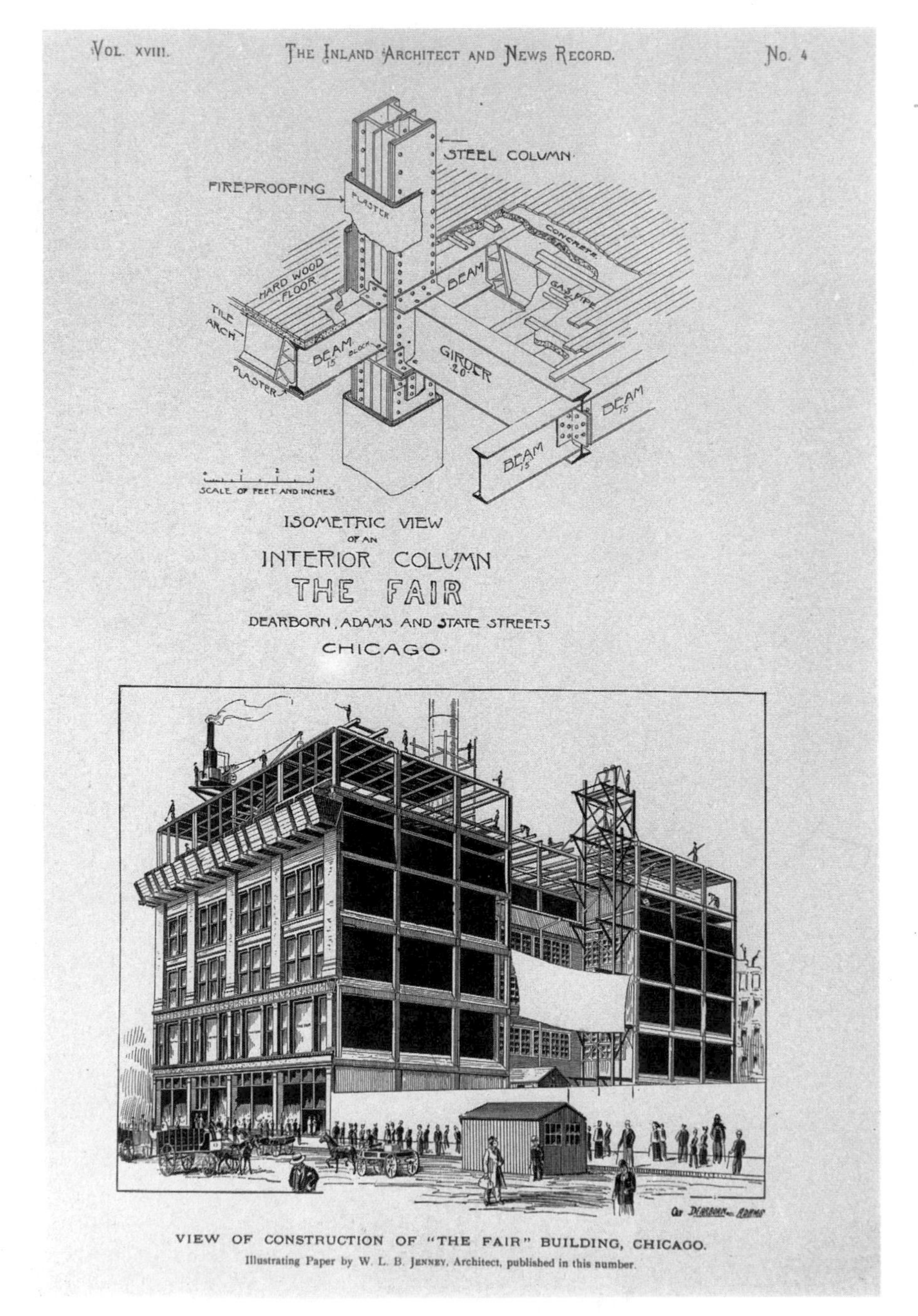

and Braque in 1907 with the development of Cubism. Abstract art replaced representative art and this conceptual, intellectual approach to design was of paramount importance to the development of the new architecture in the twentieth century.

## THE DEVELOPMENT OF IRON

Iron production was revolutionized in the early eighteenth century when coke was first used instead of charcoal for smelting iron ore. Previously the poor quality of the iron had restricted its use to items such as chains and tie-bars for supporting arches, vaults and walls. With the improvement in smelting it was now possible to make cast-iron beams, columns and girders. During the nineteenth century further advances were made, notably Bessemer's process for converting iron into steel (1856) which gave the material greater commercial viability.

The structural potential of iron was soon recognized and it was rapidly adopted for the building of bridges, its tensile strength far greater than that of stone or timber. The first bridge to be constructed of iron was the Iron Bridge, Coalbrookdale, Shropshire (1779) with a main span of 100 feet. A century later Brooklyn Bridge, New York (1870-83) achieved a main span of 1596 feet. The use of iron in architecture developed more slowly. By 1800 a complete internal iron skeleton had been developed in industrial architecture replacing traditional timber beams, but it generally remained concealed. Apart from its low cost, the appeal of iron as a building material lay in its strength, its resistance to fire and its potential to span vast areas. As a result iron became increasingly popular as a structural material for more traditional forms of architecture during the nineteenth century. Nash used iron in the construction of the Brighton Pavilion (1815) and Barry replaced the traditional timber with cast iron for the roofs of the Houses of Parliament (1837-67), but it was invariably concealed.

Significantly, the exposed use of iron occurred mainly in the new building types spawned by the Industrial Revolution; in factories, warehouses, commercial offices, exhibition halls and railroad stations, where its practical advantages far outweighed its lack of status. The use of iron on the façade of buildings was pioneered in America, where it was used on commercial buildings in direct imitation of stone. Designers of the railroad stations of the new age explored the potential of iron, covering huge areas with spans which surpassed the great vaults of medieval cathedrals. Paxton's hall to house the Great Exhibition, London (1851), the Crystal Palace, covered an area 1848 feet by 408 feet in prefabricated units of glass set in iron frames. The Paris Exhibition (1889) included both the widest span and greatest height achieved so far with the Halle des Machines, spanning 362 feet, and the Eiffel Tower 1000 feet high. However, these achievements were mocked by the artistic élite of Paris as expensive and ugly follies. Iron, despite its structural advantages, had little aesthetic status.

The exposure of an iron structure in the more traditional fields of architecture was slower to develop. Viollet-le-Duc's innovatory attitude is shown by the recommendation in his book, *Entretiens* (1872), of the undisguised use of iron in his Gothic constructions. Exposed iron columns were used effectively by Labrouste in the interior of his Bibliothèque Ste Geneviève, Paris (1843). However Viollet-le-Duc and Labrouste simply experimented with the structural potential of iron. Stylistically it imitated the stone it replaced.

Innovations in style reflecting the new structures developed in the new architecture of

**Below:** Sullivan, Wainwright Building, St Louis, Missouri, 1890. Heavy corner piers offer visual reassurance but conceal the iron structure beneath.

**Above:** Jenney, Home Insurance Building, Chicago, Illinois, 1884-5 (demolished 1931). Despite a skeleton-steel frame, this building emulates a Renaissance *palazzo* with horizontal divisions articulated by classical pilasters, a fitting image for the merchants of Florence or Chicago.

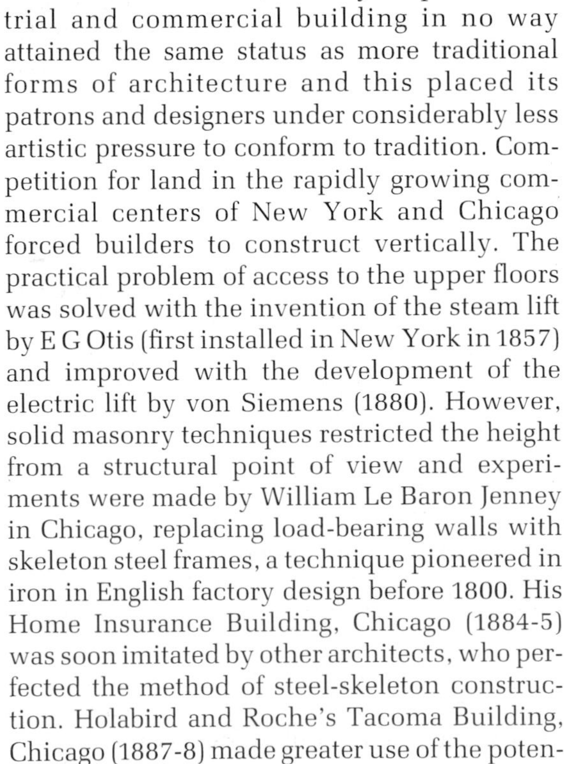

commercial America, the skyscraper. Industrial and commercial building in no way attained the same status as more traditional forms of architecture and this placed its patrons and designers under considerably less artistic pressure to conform to tradition. Competition for land in the rapidly growing commercial centers of New York and Chicago forced builders to construct vertically. The practical problem of access to the upper floors was solved with the invention of the steam lift by E G Otis (first installed in New York in 1857) and improved with the development of the electric lift by von Siemens (1880). However, solid masonry techniques restricted the height from a structural point of view and experiments were made by William Le Baron Jenney in Chicago, replacing load-bearing walls with skeleton steel frames, a technique pioneered in iron in English factory design before 1800. His Home Insurance Building, Chicago (1884-5) was soon imitated by other architects, who perfected the method of steel-skeleton construction. Holabird and Roche's Tacoma Building, Chicago (1887-8) made greater use of the potential of the metal frame, which eliminated the need for supporting walls, allowing far greater areas of fenestration. However, the early skyscrapers, although innovatory in their structure, were decorated in the style of the traditional solid masonry blocks, conforming to the classical tradition in their emphasis on the horizontal divisions between the floors breaking up the vertical elements.

Burnham and Root's Monadnock Building, Chicago, Illinois (1891) marks an important development in style. Although not technically a skyscraper, but a solid masonry structure, the building is devoid of any superficial ornament and it has a strong vertical emphasis. Louis Sullivan is generally credited with the development of vertical emphasis in steel-framed architecture with the Wainwright Building, St Louis, Missouri (1890-1). Although the exterior decoration does not precisely reflect the actual structure, the vertical elements break up the horizontal divisions and, symbolically, it is the structural vertical elements that are unadorned, whereas the traditionally dominating, horizontal elements are heavily decorated. Sullivan's masterpiece is the Guaranty Building, Buffalo, New York (1894-5). Like the Wainwright Building, Sullivan separates the lower two levels into a solid plain block, separated from the more decorated verticality of the upper part of the building. This is visually reassuring, as are the heavy corner piers but as Sullivan explained in an essay of 1896, 'The Tall Office Building Artistically Considered,' it reflects the function of the offices inside. He divided the functional areas of the building into five levels: the basement for the power

**Right:** Sullivan, Guaranty Building, Buffalo, New York, 1894-5. A classical façade in a modern idiom. Sullivan adapts an arched loggia, crowned by a cornice, to give classical status to this new palace of commerce.

**Left:** Burnham & Root, Reliance Building, Chicago, Illinois, 1894-5. An important step in skyscraper design with a repeated horizontal unit and few historical references.

plants, two levels immediately above ground with public access for banks and other facilities, a fourth level of indefinite height, for offices, and the whole crowned by an attic. His design clearly reflects the varying functions of the different levels.

The importance of the Chicago School and the development of the skyscraper was considerable to the modern movement. The problem of increasing office space was solved with a structure developed from modern materials, its form dictated by functional requirements and its decoration breaking away from historical tradition. It is no coincidence that this development took place in America. America was less hampered by tradition than Europe, her booming industry the basis of her new wealth and the skyscraper the symbol of that achievement.

HOME LIFE

## INNOVATION AND TRADITION: THE DOMESTIC REVIVAL

The small private house has long been a forum for the introduction of new ideas. It is relatively cheap and is not justifiably subject to the same popular praise and blame as public architecture. During the late nineteenth century new aesthetics were developed in the design of private houses in response to the rise of the middle classes and a new type of prosperous and well-educated patron.

The developing interest in the vernacular on the part of these new patrons, partly inspired by the Arts and Crafts movement, was a direct criticism of the eclectic styles employed by the very rich, who preferred to imitate the wealthy of the past. Philip Webb's Red House, Bexleyheath (1859), built for William Morris, started a trend which lasted well into the twentieth century, characterized by the use of brick or other local building materials, the simplification of traditional decorative forms and the development of a modern decorative style which related to contemporary society. In America architects followed the English lead, designing houses using their own traditional materials such as half-timbering and shingled walls, with an emphasis on simplification and a lack of unnecessary ornament. Their really original contribution lay in the development of unusual and asymmetrical plans, emphasizing the importance of designing the interior of homes for the inhabitants.

**Above:** McKim, Mead & White, Pennsylvania Station, New York City, 1906-10. Roman Bath architecture in iron and glass explores the structural potential of these materials to imitate a solid masonry structure.

Parallel with this development of a new style in domestic architecture was a strong preference for tradition in the public commissions of those same architects. This pattern is common to much early twentieth-century architecture and reflects the differing demands of various types of patron. McKim, Mead and White's Isaac Bell Jr House, Newport, Rhode Island (1881-2) has a totally asymmetrical plan, with large areas centred on a hall, but their Boston Public Library (1888-95) is a masterpiece in the Beaux-Arts classical tradition, with little attempt to create a modern style. Sullivan,

**Left:** Sullivan, Auditorium Building, Chicago, Illinois, 1887-9. This project involved an office building, hotel and opera house, and was designed to echo the grandeur of Ancient Rome.

**Far left:** Gilbert, Woolworth Building, New York City, 1913. Gothic became a popular style for the skyscraper with its vertical emphasis and traditional appeal.

**Above:** General view of World's Columbian Exposition, Chicago, Illinois, 1893. The committee in charge opted for a classical style for the entire exhibition, constructed out of plaster and timber.

whose innovations in the design of the skyscraper have already been discussed, shows a preference for tradition in his other projects. His Auditorium Building, Chicago (1887-9), was designed to include not only an auditorium, but also office space and a hotel to finance the venture. The façade follows the format of a Renaissance palace with heavily rusticated lower levels and arches supported on piers articulating the central section of the building. His Transportation Building for the World's Columbian Exposition, Chicago (1893) was noticeably different from the general classical flavor of the rest of the buildings in the exhibition, suggesting Romanesque inspiration for its huge arched entrance.

Charles Voysey was an important and influential late Arts and Crafts architect who developed a highly simplified and modern style. His finest work was Broadleys, a house by Lake Windermere, Westmorland (1898-9). It was traditional but without any of the medievalism of Webb and Morris. The simplicity of his interpretation of traditional features such as mullion and transom windows, illustrates the modernity of his approach. His own house at Chorleywood, Hertfordshire (1899-1900) has a characteristically heavy horizontal emphasis and the interior is very plain, with white walls and contrasting woodwork. His elegant and simple approach to design was an important influence in the development of the modern movement.

Parallel developments were made in the United States by Frank Lloyd Wright. Wright had trained in Sullivan's office in Chicago and

set up on his own in 1893, starting a career that produced some of the most original architecture of the twentieth century. His earliest buildings show the influence of the vernacular movement, but Wright's conscious realization of the necessity of developing a modern style soon showed. F L Wright believed in a new architecture that was an expression of the new and powerful American democracy, not based on styles of other cultures, and he recognized the powerful potential of the new industrial materials, iron and concrete, designing a concrete church for the Unitarians in Oak Park, Illinois (1906). His early buildings made important innovations in the development of the ground plan, already anticipated in the private commissions of McKim, Mead and White, and the synthesis of the plan with the elevation. His emphasis on horizontality is similar to that of Charles Voysey.

His first house, the Winslow House, River Forest, Illinois (1893) has a heavy overhanging roof, and the decoration of the upper story with terracotta panels shows the influence of Sullivan. Shortly after this Wright developed his concept of the 'Prairie House,' a spacious family house set in the greenery of the Chicago suburbs. One of the earliest Prairie Houses was the Ward W Willits House, Highland Park, Illinois (1902) and it typifies his desire to compose a well-organized whole, which he described as 'streamlined.' He believed that layout should respond to function rather than to outmoded traditional requirements and he admitted to the role of Froebel blocks in his development of spatial complexity and rhythm. The Willits House was designed on an open plan and broke down traditional barriers between the interior and exterior of the building. The lack of ornamentation was extremely unconventional at the time and illustrates the innovatory quality of Wright's early architecture. His Larkin Building, Buffalo, New York (1904-5) was designed as a simple monumental block, with a highly simplified approach to classical ornament which anticipated postwar developments in this direction. Wright's masterpiece from this period was undoubtedly the Robie House, Oak Park, Illinois (1909), which showed how far he had moved from the traditional and revivalist styles of his contemporaries. He deliberately simplified the essential parts of the house to bare necessities and composed them on an open plan, relating the building to its site with heavy horizontal elements. Again, the almost complete lack of decoration and use of a single material sets the house far apart from historical traditions.

**Above:** Wright, Ward W Willits House, Highland Park, Illinois, 1902. One of Wright's 'Prairie Houses,' spacious, modern houses set in the suburbs of Chicago for the wealthy businessman, whose conventional appearance belies Wright's modern achievements.

**Left:** Bacon, Lincoln Memorial, Washington DC, 1912-22. The choice of a traditional style reflects the reverence for Lincoln. Its combination of a Greek temple with a Roman attic suggests both democracy and triumph.

**Above:** Wright, W H Winslow House, River Forest, Illinois, 1893. This early house with its heavy overhanging cornice and simplicity of form shows the originality, which marked Wright's long career.

**Below:** Wright, W H Winslow House, River Forest, Illinois, 1893. Wright's early training in Sullivan's office shows in his rare use of ornament and traditional features.

In 1909 there occurred the first of a number of breaks in Wright's long career. He left his wife and the United States for Europe and settled in Italy with his mistress. There he prepared a portfolio of his drawings, which were published in Germany in 1910. These drawings had an enormous influence on the development of German architecture and, inevitably, on the beginning of the modern movement. However, his somewhat spicy private life had an adverse effect on his career. Initially commissions were difficult on his return to the United States in 1911 and he spent his enforced leisure designing a new home, Taliesin, for himself and his mistress, in Spring Green, Wisconsin. It provided an ideal environment for Wright, combining farm buildings, studio and living quarters. The informality of the layout of the complex, which responded to the geography of the site, marks an important step beyond the Prairie Houses. In 1914 tragedy struck Wright. Shortly after the completion of Taliesin, while Wright was away on business, one of the servants ran amok, killed his mistress and her two children and set fire to the house, partially destroying it. The following year he left the United States again, this time to take up a commission in Japan to build the Imperial Hotel, Tokyo (1916-22).

Californian architects were also experimenting with new approaches to design, notably in the works of the brothers Charles and Henry Greene. Although less conceptual than Wright's Prairie Houses, the Greenes' Gamble House, Pasadena, California (1908) shows the same interest in the relationship between interior and exterior space. Irving Gill, who had trained with Adler and Sullivan in Chicago, was much influenced by the Spanish tradition of architecture in California and combined this interest with a modern abstract design in his Walter Luther Dodge House, Los Angeles (1916) in a way that was comparable to the

**Above:** Wright, Frederick C Robie House, Oak Park, Illinois, 1909. A harmonious balance of horizontal and vertical elements conveys a reassuring sense of solidity in this startlingly modern building.

**Left:** Wright, Frederick C Robie House, Oak Park, Illinois, 1909. Wright's interior use of space is unique.

**Above:** Charles & Henry Greene, Gamble House, Pasadena, California, 1908. Verandas, pitched roofs and shingling continue the vernacular tradition but the modernity of the composition sets this house apart.

recent prewar developments in Austria and Germany.

The particular socialist philosophy of the Arts and Crafts movement to rehumanize society also found an outlet in the paternalistic philanthropy of a few industrialists, such as George Cadbury and W H Lever (afterward Lord Leverhulme), who commissioned architects to design the first garden cities for their workers at Bournville and Port Sunlight respectively. The idea of well-designed workers' housing is of crucial importance to the development of the modern movement. Projects like these were successful and led to further developments, including Ebenezer Howard's book of town-planning, *Tomorrow* (1898), in which he expounded his theory of the garden city, with separate zones for housing, industry and public buildings and a strong emphasis on trees and grass, in direct contrast to the grim, dark, and muddled industrial cities which had developed in response to capitalist requirements. His ideas had a powerful influence on architects such as Garnier and, later, Le Corbusier. In 1903 Howard formed a public company, appropriately called 'First Garden City Limited,' to finance the project and Letchworth, the first garden city, was started in 1904. It was followed by others, notably Hampstead Garden Suburb (1907). In the Arts and Crafts tradition, the houses were not uniformly designed and were arranged informally beside roads with broad verges planted with trees and even herbaceous borders.

## ART NOUVEAU

Art Nouveau was a romantic and highly decorative movement which swept through Europe and America between 1890 and 1910. Stylistically it developed out of the Arts and Crafts movement in England but without the same socialist ideals. In historical terms the Arts and Crafts movement and Art Nouveau bridge the gap between the eclecticism of the nineteenth century and the modern movement. Both movements are part of the dissatisfaction with contemporary reliance on historical styles and illustrate the search for new modes of artistic expression.

The name *Art Nouveau* comes from the title given by Samuel Bing to his shop in Paris which was opened in December 1895. In Germany the style was known as *Jugendstil*, so-called after the eponymous journal, which first appeared in 1896. In Austria it was called *Sezessionstil*, after the Viennese Sezession group of painters and architects, founded in 1897. The style affected all the arts, especially architecture and the decorative arts and it was characterized by the use of sinuous, slender and asymmetrical curves which tended to form floral patterns in Belgium and France, but geometrical patterns in Scotland and Austria. There are strong, but subconscious links between Art Nouveau and eighteenth-century Rococo. Both styles emphasize the decorative rather than the structural, both attempt to break away from the formality of traditional ornament by abandoning symmetry in favor of a more naturalistic style, and both are followed by an abrupt return to rigid rules.

The early designs of Art Nouveau appeared unconsciously in the decorative designs of the Arts and Crafts movement. Traditionally, the first work is taken to be Mackmurdo's cover for a book on Wren's City of London churches (1883). Arthur Mackmurdo was a member of the Arts and Crafts movement and, initially at least, the new fashion was just a development within this style. Many English Arts and Crafts designers, such as Voysey, produced designs during the 1880s which, with the benefit of hindsight, we can describe as Art Nouveau and these were a major influence on European decorative arts. Emile Gallé began to produce his glassware from 1884 onward and his influence spread to the United States, where Tiffany started his Favrile glass in 1893.

Art Nouveau was also the inspiration for Victor Horta's design for the Tassel House, Brussels (1892). Behind a plain façade, the interior of the house shows exceptional novelty in its decorative features. Horta's use of iron as the material of decorative detail was an important aspect of Art Nouveau. Its flexibility and fineness made it ideal for the twisted and curved shapes which characterized the style. There is no attempt to disguise the iron, and its decorative potential is exploited to the full. The fluid and sinuous patterns of the staircase are inlaid into the floor and painted on the walls in a unity of decoration characteristic of Art Nou-

**Left:** Horta, Tassel House, Brussels, Belgium, 1892. The undisguised use of iron in this domestic interior was innovatory, illustrating the preferences of the patron, Tassel, who was an engineer, and Horta's genius for exploiting the decorative potential of iron.

**Right:** Horta, Atelier Horta, Brussels, Belgium 1898. The elaborate use of iron breaks completely with traditional balcony design as classical columns mutate into naturalistic forms.

veau. Horta built a number of other private houses in Brussels, including the Hôtel Solvay (1894) and the Maison Winssinger (1895). His most important commission was the Maison du Peuple (1896), the headquarters of the Belgian Socialist Party, which consisted of an enormous conference hall, a large café and a meeting area, as well as offices. Both the exterior and interior display the exposed metal structure, combining concave and convex curves reflecting the shape of the site, and the ironwork is elaborate and extremely fanciful in decoration.

Horta's innovations in the Tassel House were taken up by Belgian architects, notably by Henri van der Velde. He trained as a painter but rejected this path in favor of the Arts and Crafts movement, designing tapestries and furniture before embarking upon a career in architecture in 1895. Van der Velde's first building was his own house at Uccle, near Brussels (1895), which followed Voysey and the Arts and Crafts tradition of unity of design for both the building and its interior furnishings. He completely fitted out the house with furniture, cutlery, curtains, dinner service and even clothes for himself and his wife, to harmonize with the

**Right:** Guimard, Métro station, Paris, France, 1899. Guimard blurs the traditional border between structure and decoration, creating a composition of naturalistic forms.

building. The success of this house inspired Samuel Bing to commission van der Velde in 1896 to fit out four rooms in the shop he had opened in Paris, L'Art Nouveau.

In France, the style set by Horta and brought to Paris by van der Velde was developed by Hector Guimard. Guimard's best-known works are the Paris Métro stations, designed between 1899 and 1904. They are all built in iron and are perhaps the best illustration of the virtuosity of the style. In his private commissions Guimard, like Horta, showed his innovation in the decorative metalwork rather than in the structure. The apartment building, Castel Béranger, Paris (1895-7), displays Guimard's ability to use combinations of materials, including an ornate metal gate, terracotta panels in the entrance hall, bizarre cast-iron details of naturalistic inspiration and a staircase wall composed of small double-curved glass panels whose irregularity enhances the profusion and variety of forms. The flamboyance of his style was used to great effect in the now-demolished Humbert de Romans building in Paris (1902), where the interior auditorium had curved structural members far more ambitious than those of Horta's Maison du Peuple.

**Left:** Guimard, Castel Béranger, Paris, France, 1895-7. The elaborate decoration of this gateway uses sinuous naturalistic forms composed in a deliberately asymmetric and anticlassical manner.

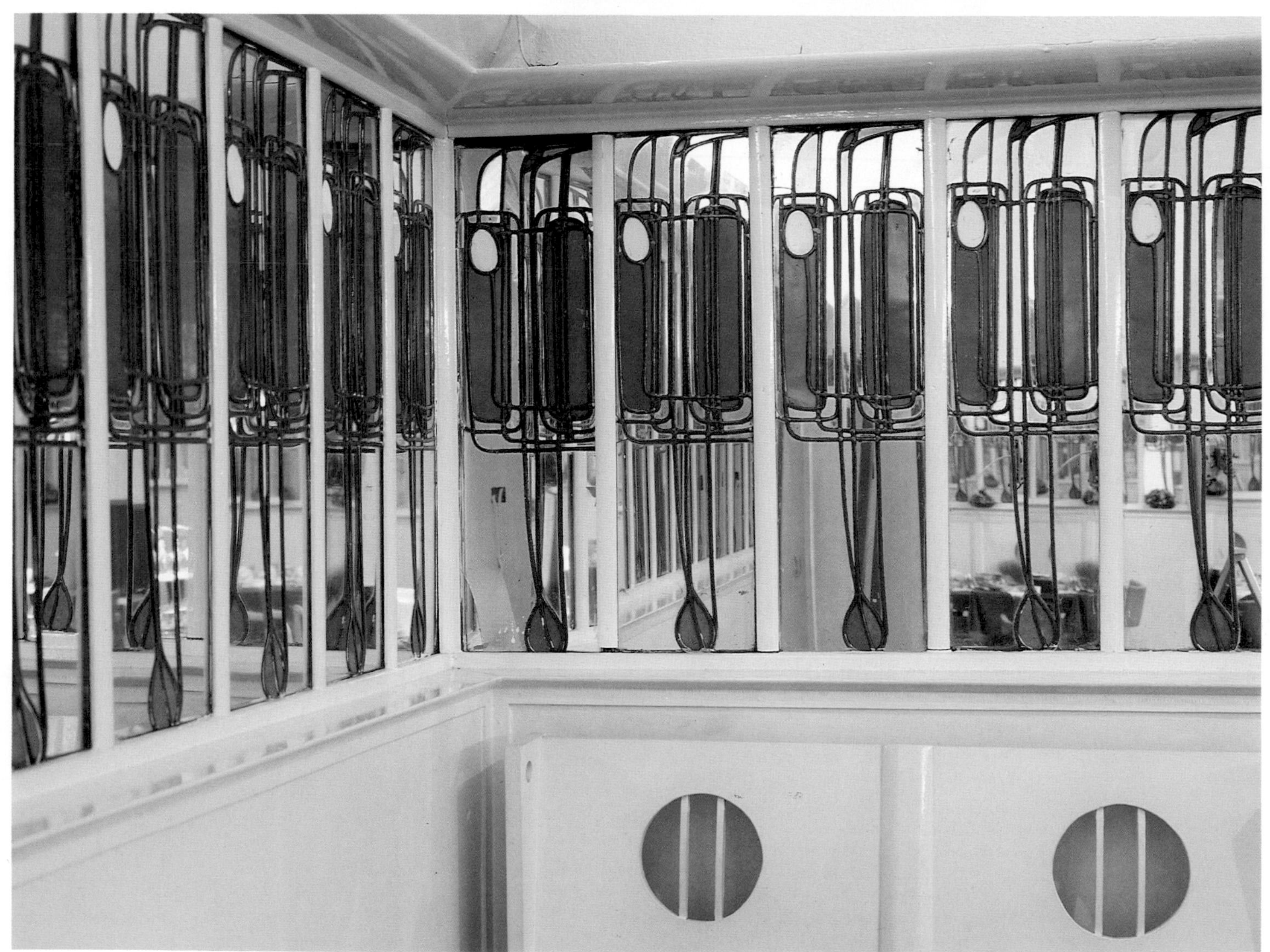

**Below:** Mackintosh, Willow Tea Rooms, Sauciehall Street, Glasgow, Scotland, 1903. The elegant and graceful decor shows a restrained interpretation of Art Nouveau, preferred by Mackintosh and his Scottish patron.

**Above:** Jourdain, Samaritaine Department Store, Paris, France, 1905. One of the most elaborate of the Art Nouveau department stores, with extensive glazed areas supported in the steel frame which was decorated with elaborate ironwork and ceramic tiles.

The Paris Exhibition of 1900 was the first international and public showing of the new style and, ironically, the beginning of its downfall into vulgar commercialization. The Pavilion Art Nouveau, commissioned by Samuel Bing, was designed by Georges de Feure and filled with Art Nouveau artifacts. Art Nouveau, which obtained its name from a shop in the first place, seemed eminently suitable for department stores which were opening up all over Europe and North America. Its emphasis on the decorative, lightness and frivolity, the cheapness of the materials involved and its popular appeal made it an obvious success with the patrons of stores such as the Tietz Department Store, Berlin, by Sehring (1898), the Carson, Pirie, and Scott Store, Chicago, by Sullivan (1899-1904), Harrods, London, by Stevens and Mund (1901-5) and the Samaritaine Dept Store, Paris, by Jourdain (1905).

Outside France the style developed less dramatically. August Endell designed his Studio Elvira, Munich (1897-8), now destroyed, as a simple rectangular façade with asymmetric window spacing, reminiscent of Voysey. However, the application of a huge plaster ornament to the façade, looking something like a mermaid and a dragon, gave the building an unmistakably Art Nouveau flavor. Endell also designed other buildings in the same style, such as the Buntes Theater, Berlin (1901).

Art Nouveau did not really take hold in England, but in Scotland a group of artist-craftsmen based in Glasgow, established a variant of the style under Charles Rennie Mackintosh. Mackintosh was commissioned to design the Glasgow School of Art (completed 1909). His decorative use of metal on the façade was clearly influenced by Art Nouveau, but the façade itself does not approach the playfulness of the French and Belgian versions. His interior decoration was much closer in style. In 1897 he was commissioned to design the interiors, including the furnishings, of a chain of tearooms in Glasgow, which have a sense of frivolity lacking in the Glasgow School of Art. His later works show the development of his style away from the decorative and toward the abstract. The interior of the library of the Glasgow School of Art (1907-9) was constructed on a traditional plan with nave and side aisles, but it is hugely simplified into plain horizontal and vertical elements, allowing a variety of interesting perspectives. His concern for the construction of space had become far more important than decoration, and the curve, which was never very prevalent in his earlier works, had completely disappeared.

The comparative austerity of Mackintosh's style was influential in Vienna, contributing to the rejection of Art Nouveau around 1907. The foundation of the Sezession group in Vienna in

1897 which seceded from the artistic establishment of the city, gave impetus to the development of Art Nouveau in Austria, particularly in the works of its leading personality, Gustav Klimt. His highly decorative and two-dimensional style of painting was influenced by the works of Aubrey Beardsley and Jan Toorop, as well as by Mackintosh. Otto Wagner, another member of the group, was commissioned to design a number of Vienna Stadtbahn railroad stations between 1894 and 1901, but in comparison to Guimard's Métro stations they are very restrained. Another of the prominent members of the group was Joseph Olbrich, who designed the Sezessionhalle, Vienna (1898), a gallery to house the exhibitions of the group. The decorative openwork metal dome contrasts with the massivity of the rest of the structure, illustrating the parallel between the Viennese architects and Sullivan and Mackintosh in their juxtaposition of massive structures with delicate Art Nouveau decoration. This contrasts with the French and the Belgians, whose concern for structure was often limited to its use as a vehicle for carrying the decoration. In 1899 Olbrich was invited to Darmstadt, Germany, to work for Grand Duke Ernst Ludwig von Hesse. The colony of artists gathered there formed the focal point for the reaction to Art Nouveau. This reaction was influenced by their comparison of the Art Nouveau styles of the French and the Belgians with that of Mackintosh, whose designs had been requested by the Sezession group for their exhibition in 1900.

The works of the Spanish architect Antoni Gaudí, traditionally considered part of the Art Nouveau movement, conform to this interpretation in date alone. His highly individual style belongs in a class of his own. Unlike Horta and Guimard, Gaudí's architecture is concerned with space. It uses many historical features, particularly medieval and Arabic; styles traditional to Spain. Gaudí combined them in a form that was entirely his own, and in many ways he is the only architect of the first part of the twentieth century to achieve a completely modern style.

His first commission was to complete the church of La Sagrada Familia, Barcelona,

**Below:** Neatby, Harrods Meat Hall, London, England, 1901. Although more restrained in England, Art Nouveau was still the fashionable choice for decorating new store interiors. Harrods Meat Hall is covered in glazed ceramic tiles to provide an attractive, practical environment.

**Right:** Gaudí, Parque Güell, Barcelona, Spain, 1900-14. Built for Count Güell, this house looks almost human with its jutting bay window beneath two 'eyes.'

**Far right:** Gaudí, Casa Batlló, Barcelona, Spain, 1904-6. Decorated for a wealthy textile merchant, José Batlló, the real windows can be seen in the façade contrasting strongly with Gaudí's amorphous balconies and window surrounds.

**Below:** Gaudí, Church of La Sagrada Familia, Barcelona, Spain, 1884. The traditional towers which grace the west front of a Gothic cathedral are here, totally transformed into a modern idiom.

which had been started in 1882. He worked on the church from 1884 to his death in 1926 and its development from a relatively ordinary neo-Gothic church into one of the most spectacular buildings of the twentieth century expresses Gaudí's own stylistic evolution. Initially, at ground level, he adhered to the traditional three portals of a Gothic church but covered them in naturalistic ornament quite unlike their prototypes. Above the portals rise another traditional feature, the towers, again treated in a totally novel way and only remotely Gothic. They are topped with finials constructed from multiplanar surfaces and decorated with brightly colored mosaics. The whole conception is an expression of Gaudí's extraordinary individuality.

His major secular buildings date from around 1905 and they show the clear influence of Art Nouveau, but lack all the restraint showed by Horta and Guimard in their treatment of the façade. Gaudí used the curve for the construction and the decoration of the building, a development which had only been hinted at in the least restrained buildings of

45

**Above:** Gaudí, Casa Milá, Barcelona, Spain, 1905-7. An apartment block whose façade seems to be modeled in clay, with undulating waves of masonry decorated with 'seaweed' balconies.

Guimard, his Métro stations. The extent to which the curve was incorporated into the building went far beyond Art Nouveau and anticipates the Expressionist movement in postwar architecture. These private commissions include fantastic houses for a variety of wealthy patrons, including his main patron, Count Güell. Through Güell he met José Batlló, a wealthy textile merchant who commissioned him in 1904 to remodel an existing building to provide not only business premises but also a family flat. The resulting creation suggests inspiration from an underwater grotto and is quite unique. The façade of the Casa Milá is even more extraordinary and its plan is remarkable for its complete lack of symmetry, with irregularly shaped rooms grouped around an equally irregular courtyard. It is difficult to find a right-angle in either plan or elevation.

Art Nouveau was a short-lived but intense movement and its original novelty rapidly deteriorated into a commercial exploitation of the style. However, its achievements should not be ignored. A style was developed which exploited the decorative potential of new materials and which deliberately set out to cut some of the links that bound architecture to the styles of the past.

## THE REACTION TO ART NOUVEAU

In 1908 the Austrian architect Adolf Loos published an essay entitled *Ornament und Verbrechen*, 'Ornament and Crime,' which proposed that architecture should be considered beautiful in proportion to the degree of usefulness it attained. Beauty related to function was one of Sullivan's tenets, and Loos' visit to Chicago had clearly influenced him. The idea that beauty was inherent in the structure of buildings was also expressed by H P Berlage, a Dutch architect who had remained

**Left:** Olbrich, Hochzeitsturm, Darmstadt, West Germany, 1907-8. The 'wedding tower' surmounted by five organ pipes retains the curved form of Art Nouveau but their solidity shows how Olbrich's style had developed.

outside the Art Nouveau movement. In an attack on what he saw as the superficialities of Art Nouveau, he emphasized that architecture was the creation of space, not the designing of façades, and that the walls articulating this space should be unadorned so as not to detract from their beauty by the addition of ornament. Experiments in the relationship between space and form by Wright in his early houses has already been discussed, but it is important to remember that these developments were parallel to similar, if less original, developments in Europe which are crucial to the growth of the modern movement.

Some of the most ardent Art Nouveau architects developed away from the decorative toward the spatial after 1900. August Endell published a book on the emotional qualities of building proportions in 1898, illustrated with plain-fronted buildings, not unlike his Studio Elvira in Munich but without its bizarre decoration. Van der Velde, who moved to Germany in 1899, remodeled the Folkwang Museum, Hagen (1900-2) with a far more restrained and linear interpretation of Art Nouveau. In 1901 he moved to Weimar under the patronage of Grand Duke Wilhelm Ernst of Saxe-Weimar and in 1906, as head of the Weimar School of Arts and Crafts, designed a new building for the school, which shows none of his earlier Art Nouveau preferences.

The main centers of reaction to Art Nouveau were Vienna and Darmstadt, where a Viennese architect, Olbrich, had the major influence on the artists' colony set up there by Grand Duke Ernst Ludwig von Hesse in 1899. As van der Velde, Olbrich's rejection of Art Nouveau took the form of simplifying the decorative style. He designed houses for some of the members of the colony, including one for Julius Glückert (1901), a solid building decorated with a variety of window forms. Its omega-shaped entrance door betrays his preference for Art Nouveau curves but the linearity of interpretation emphasizes his strong links with Mackintosh.

**Below:** Wagner, Steinhof church, Vienna, Austria, 1905-7: a classical temple with dome and porch. Only the modernity of the decorative details distinguishes it from the Baroque.

Olbrich's main assistant was Peter Behrens, who trained as a painter, but turned to architecture and interior decoration. In 1901 he designed his own house in the colony, which demonstrates the influence of Olbrich. In his description of the house, Behrens shows how he developed away from Art Nouveau by comparing previous efforts to relieve the bareness of utilitarian objects with ornamentation and his own recognition of the beauty inherent in functional design.

In Vienna three architects, Otto Wagner, Josef Hoffmann and the main critic of Art Nouveau, Adolf Loos, developed a simple and expensive style largely under the patronage of the wealthy élite, following a similar pattern to Gaudí in Barcelona. As early as 1894, Wagner had praised horizontal lines, flat roofs, lack of decoration and the use of steel, believing that beauty in architecture lay in structure not decoration. His Post Office Savings Bank (1905) shows his preference for new materials and has a strong classical simplicity, very much in contrast to his earlier works.

After Olbrich had left for Darmstadt, Hoffmann took over as architect to the wealthy Hohe Warte suburb in Vienna, designing four houses there during the years 1901-5, showing the influence of Voysey. His first major public commission was the Purkersdorf Sanatorium near Vienna (1903). It consisted of a simplified block, plastered in white, with a flat roof, and the only decoration was a band of blue and white tiles emphasizing the structure of the building. Hoffmann's masterpiece was the Palais Stoclet, an elegant and graceful version of the Sanatorium, with the same white walls,

**Above:** Van der Velde, Art School, Weimar, East Germany, 1906. A functional design with large areas of fenestration, lacking the decorative emphasis in his earlier works.

**Right:** Behrens, Behrens' House, Darmstadt, West Germany, 1901. Behrens' early work shows the influence of Art Nouveau in the curved windows and the decoration of the white walls with strips of green tiles.

**Above:** Wagner, Post Office Savings Bank, Vienna, Austria, 1905. The unadorned interior, constructed in metal and glass, has a grace and elegance typical of the Viennese architecture of the period.

but here they are faced with marble and the outline is delineated with thin metal bands more appropriate to the status of the patron. In contrast, the interior is considerably more luxurious and includes a dining-room with wall decoration of mosaics by Klimt, made up of glass, enamel, metal and semiprecious stones. The emphasis of the building is on fine materials and proportion, devoid of the moldings and sculptural ornament of Art Nouveau.

Loos was opposed to the élitism of Hoffmann's style, characterized by grace and elegance. In 1906 he founded the Free School of Architecture in Vienna in order to spread his more puritanical ideals. The bulk of his work up to 1914 involved the redecoration and remodeling of the interiors of shops, flats and bars. His use of simplified classical forms is evident in the interior of the American (now Kärntner) Bar, Vienna (1907), which has a heavily coffered ceiling, and his concern for internal space can be seen in his careful positioning of mirrors above the high mahogany wainscoting to disguise its small size. His major work was the Steiner House, Vienna (1910), one of the first private houses to be built of reinforced concrete. It also represents a turning point in architectural style, with its flat roof, unadorned and solid exterior and emphasis on horizontality, stressed by the windows. In the planning of the interior Loos shows interest in spatial composition, and his later houses develop the idea of the split-level interior, for example in the Moller House, Vienna (1928). Loos' originality was not immediately influential, but his work marks an important step which would be recognized in the 1920s.

Outside Germany and Austria, other architects were developing along similar lines. Berlage, like Voysey in England, attempted to

**Below:** Hoffmann, Palais Stoclet, Brussels, Belgium, 1905-11. An austere building enlivened by a variety of angles.

**Above:** Loos, Steiner House, Vienna, Austria, 1910. A work of great importance in the development of the modern movement, eliminating non-structural elements from the façade, a major step toward the rationalism of the interwar years.

interpret the vernacular tradition in a modern idiom. His first important commission was the Stock Exchange Building, Amsterdam (1897-1903), which used unembellished brickwork on the interior walls, enlivened by simple stone moldings to enhance colonnaded balconies around the central open space. In 1911 Berlage went to Chicago and his later works show the influence of Sullivan. Berlage's influence on the next generation of Dutch architects was considerable, especially his use of unornamented brick and emphasis on structural honesty. In the countries where Art Nouveau had only a minor influence, such as Holland and Scandinavia, the ideas of the Arts and Crafts movement were more readily adopted, the traditional English elements being replaced by indigenous materials and styles. Prewar Scandinavian architecture also saw a developing interest in spatial forms, combined with a use of traditional materials. Eliel Saarinen's early works show the influence of the Arts and Crafts movement, notably in the Villa Hvitträsk, near Helsinki (1902), and his Helsinki Railway Station (1905) is an elegant structure with many eclectic but simplified features.

## CONCRETE IN ARCHITECTURE

The vast scale of Ancient Roman architecture owes much to their exploration of the potential of concrete. Knowledge of this material disappeared during the Middle Ages and was only redeveloped in the eighteenth century. In 1774 it was used as a base for the Eddystone Lighthouse, in the English Channel, and during the 1830s mass concrete was first used in the construction of houses. Its resistance to fire and water, its comparative cheapness and its potential for spanning large areas gave it a useful role, but it could not compete initially with the status of traditional building materials.

Experiments to improve the strength of concrete by combining it with steel began in the 1860s in France and America. In 1861 François Coignet developed a technique for reinforcing it with iron mesh, and in 1892 François Hennebique submitted the first patent for steel reinforcement of concrete. In 1895 he completed the spinning mill at Tourcoing, which used exposed concrete to frame large areas of glass. In 1897 Anatole de Baudot, a pupil of Viollet-le-Duc, built the church of St Jean-de-Montmartre, Paris, using concrete to create a neo-Gothic structure in much the same way as Viollet-le-Duc had used iron. The simplicity and austerity of the undisguised concrete is even more remarkable when one remembers that it was contemporary with Guimard's Castel Béranger. The Paris Exhibition of 1900 showed the public the possibilities of concrete

**Left:** Berlage, Stock Exchange Building, Amsterdam, the Netherlands, 1897-1903. The traditional and the modern; the brick walls support an undisguised steel frame and glass roof, in an austere version of medieval style.

**Below:** Wright, Unity Temple, Oak Park, Illinois, 1906. Wright's use of undisguised concrete is without precedent in a religious building. This unpretentious temple reflects the religious ideals of his Unitarian patrons and marks an important step in architectural history.

**Right:** Perret, 25 *bis* rue Franklin, Paris, 1902-3. The reinforced concrete framing is clearly expressed on the façade in the use of contrasting tiles. The panels between the girders are decorated with sculptural foliage ornament, showing the influence of Art Nouveau.

in buildings such as the Château d'Eau, which was built by Coignet's son. Other early uses of concrete include precast slabs on the roof of Lethaby's Church of All Saints, Brockhampton, Herefordshire, England (1900-2) and Wright's Unity Temple near Chicago (1906).

The reaction to Art Nouveau in France coincided with the development of concrete by Auguste Perret and Tony Garnier. Their major achievement was to use undisguised, reinforced concrete for both the exterior and the interior of public and private buildings and employ it in a style only partially reflecting the past, experimenting with the potential of the material itself. Perret's apartment block at 25 *bis* rue Franklin, Paris (1902-3) was the first private house constructed with reinforced concrete framing. His Beaux-Arts training shows in the classical proportions of the façade, but he expresses the modernity of the structure with contrasting tiles. His next building, a garage in the rue de Ponthieu, Paris (1905-6), was more functional, and he was not so inhibited by tradition. Here the skeleton concrete structure was exposed undisguised except for protective white paint. The advantages of the material were fully exploited both inside and on the façade where the reinforced concrete girders frame huge windows. The central window, decorated with a linear, but distinctly Art Nouveau pattern, is the only period feature.

The problems of introducing a new style into the more prestigious areas of architecture is further illustrated in the design of the Théâtre des Champs-Elysées. In 1910 van der Velde was commissioned to build the theater, and his design using a reinforced concrete structure was contracted out to the Perret firm. Perret disputed the design on structural grounds and submitted his own, which was accepted. This commission required a considerably larger structure than Perret's earlier works and it showed the potential of concrete to cover large areas. However, the façade ignored all references to the new material and, following tradition, was faced with stone in a classical, columnar style. Perret's masterpiece belongs to the postwar era. In the church of Notre-Dame at Raincy, near Paris (1922-4), he achieved one of the main aims of the Gothic cathedral builders by almost totally replacing the walls with glass. The refinement of the pierced decoration of the concrete screens holding the glass shows the superiority of concrete over stone in terms of minimizing the building's structural mass.

Tony Garnier's main contribution to architecture was his plan for an industrial city, *Cité Industrielle*, which he designed in 1901 (first exhibited 1904). Unhampered by the reality of commissions or the requirements of a patron, Garnier was able to explore the stylistic potential of concrete to fulfill the functions of a build-

**Below:** Garnier, designs from *La Cité Industrielle*, 1901. Garnier's socialist leanings are reflected in his approach to town-planning. In this Utopia, with its sports stadia and community centers, there was no need for churches, police stations or military barracks.

**Above:** Garnier, La Mouche Abattoir, Lyons, France, 1909-13. The unusual step design with flattened arches emphasizes modernity in a traditional format.

**Below:** Maillart, Tavanasa Bridge, Switzerland, 1905. Maillart combines the tension of the arched support with the weight of the flat road to create a structural and visual unity.

ing and to reject classical and all other historical styles and ornament. The houses for the population of 35,000 were to be plain cubes, arranged in groups around public garden areas which were graced with occasional statues. The houses were extremely modern in conception and anticipate the developments to be made by Le Corbusier during the 1920s. All the major buildings were to be constructed in reinforced concrete, some exhibiting important technical developments, such as the cantilevers for the administrative building and railroad station. Garnier recognized the potential of combining the forces of concrete both under compression and under tension, showing that these buildings were far in advance of anything that had been constructed at the time. Garnier was appointed Architect of the City of Lyons in 1905 and commissioned to design buildings for La Mouche, the new town outside

Lyons. Apart from the market hall, which was made of steel and glass, all the buildings are of concrete, but although simple and functional, they do not display the modernity that was apparent in his designs for *Cité Industrielle*.

The potential of reinforced concrete was exploited by other architects outside France. In the United States ferro-concrete structures were restricted up to 1895 because of their dependence on importing cement from Europe. However, important developments were made by engineers such as Ernest Ransome during the late nineteenth century. The potential of concrete was recognized in the construction of industrial and commercial buildings, notably the grain silos which were springing up all over the Midwest. These huge and unornamented structures were to be of great influence upon later architecture.

In his designs for *La Città Nuova*, Sant'Elia specified the use of concrete and the Fiat Works in Turin (begun 1915) made interesting application of the material. The Swiss engineer, Robert Maillart, was one of the first to experiment at a practical level with the combination of concrete under compression and tension, an idea which had appeared in the theoretical buildings of Garnier. Max Berg's Jahrhunderthalle, Breslau, now Wroclaw, Poland (1910-13) used a framework of reinforced concrete in a modern comment on the Pantheon. Not only is the span across the dome considerably larger, but the structural ribs which are completely hidden in the Pantheon are exposed by Berg and the stepped rows of windows light up the structure from behind, as if deliberately to emphasize the point.

The introduction of concrete followed a very similar pattern to that of steel. Although its structural merits were recognized, it lacked the status of traditional building materials, and was inevitably disguised on buildings of any importance. Attempts to develop stylistic formulas, which related more to the material than to tradition, began in commercial and industrial projects, only permeating the establishment in the 1920s. Perret, as one of Le Corbusier's teachers, had considerable practical influence on mid-century developments, and Garnier's theories and designs directly inspired Le Corbusier's work in town-planning. The view that reinforced concrete was the most important building material of the twentieth century rapidly gained ground.

**Below:** Berg, Jahrhunderthalle, Breslau (now Wroclaw), Poland, 1910-13. A modern Pantheon, with a dome span of 213 feet, (the Pantheon is 142 feet). The scale of the building reflects the technical advantages of reinforced concrete over mass concrete used by the Romans.

**Right:** Freysinnet, Orly airship hangar, Paris, 1916. Reinforced concrete was proposed as a structural material for airship hangars at Orly. These vast parabolic-vaulted spaces were far larger than anything attempted by Perret and Garnier.

## THE MACHINE AGE

The new materials, iron and concrete, were developed initially for their practical advantages over traditional building materials. Art Nouveau, a modern style which exploited the stylistic potential of these materials, had been an extravagant fad and had been followed by an abrupt return to principles of purity and simplicity in exactly the same way as the eighteenth century had reacted to the excesses of Baroque and Rococo in their ordered classicism. Prestigious architectural projects, the commissions of the establishment, remained conservative in both their choice of materials and style.

The challenge to traditionally accepted rules and restraints found an outlet in theoretical writings of the early twentieth century, which welcomed the innovations in materials, industrial advance and the growth of new attitudes to society. The desire to look forward and to develop a style which reflected the new industrial era, rather than the nonindustrial past, became paramount.

Morris' attempts to reform the arts in England had rejected the realities of industrialization. He preferred to escape back into the medieval world of craftsmanship, differing from his contemporaries only in his choice of a less glamorous historical model. However, Morris' belief in the principles of socialism were of enormous importance to future developments. The worship of industrial achievement inevitably led to a rise in the status of the workforce.

It was on the other side of the Atlantic, where the status of industrial wealth was not so hampered by an establishment whose power was based outside the realm of manufacture, that the strongest endorsement of the cult of the machine age took place. In his manifesto *The Art and Craft of the Machine* (1901), Frank Lloyd Wright was unequivocal in his praise of the machine age, foreseeing a period when railroad engines, steamships and engines of war would take the place that works of art had occupied in the past. In his book *In the Cause of Architecture* (1908) Wright made a plea for the architect to use the machine as the 'normal tool' of modern civilization, rejecting traditional structural forms and encouraging the use of the new materials, steel and concrete, as a means of creating the new democratic industrial society of the future.

Wright's theories were not taken up in America, although they were influential in Europe. His obsession with machinery found expression in the Futurist movement which published its first manifesto in February 1909. The manifesto listed 11 points, praising recklessness, energy and audacity. Echoing Wright's ideals, the Futurists considered a racing-car more beautiful than the Ancient Greek Winged Victory of Samothrace. They called for the destruction of academic institutions, such as libraries and museums and praised the beauty of industrial architecture. Initially the movement was confined to painting, and the style of the Futurists owed much to Cubist developments. However, their aim was not intellectual analysis, but rather an appeal to the emotions of the observer. Their choice of subject matter frequently related to movement as well as to industrial progress, including such titles as *The Dynamism of the Cyclist* (Umberto Boccioni, 1913) and *Suburban Trains Arriving at Paris* (Gino Severini, 1915).

In 1914 Antonio Sant'Elia exhibited a series of designs and projects under the title of *La Città Nuova*, the city of the future, and the catalogue of the exhibition inspired the leader of the Futurists, Marinetti, to invite Sant'Elia to join the group. The text of the catalogue (published later that year as the *Manifesto dell'Architettura Futurista*) illustrates the major changes that were taking place in architectural theory. Sant'Elia pledged himself to the modern age of the machine, separated from historical tradition, when he wrote that the important buildings were no longer cathedrals but hotels, railroad stations and roads, and he encouraged the construction of new cities of dynamism. He considered staircases to be obsolete, as they had been superseded by the lift, and described simple unadorned buildings built in concrete, iron and glass, responding to the needs of their function, not restricted by outdated laws. His designs show his attempt to rid architecture of its historical elements and to glorify the industrial age with designs for office blocks, apartment blocks, an electricity generating station, railroad station and an aircraft hangar.

Garnier's *Cité Industrielle*, (discussed above) first exhibited in 1904 but not published until 1918, is unashamedly socialist. His choice of title displays his belief in the cult of industrialization, but his contribution is visual rather than theoretical.

Van der Velde, whose reinforced concrete design for the Théâtre des Champs-Elysées had been criticized on technical grounds by Perret, was enthusiastic about modern materials. He contrasted the retrogressive and escapist character of the early Arts and Crafts ideals with his own doctrine of beauty inherent in machinery. He considered that the architect working in stone was no better than an engineer working in metal, recommending that the materials of the future should be iron, steel and concrete.

However, the focal point for the development of the cult of the machine age was in Germany, and the theories of Hermann Muthesius. He was an architect who had been attached to the German Embassy in London from 1896 to 1903 for the express purpose of studying English housing and he was very impressed by its simplicity and rationality. He conceived of a *Maschinenstil*, a machine style which reflected function unhampered by traditional ideals of beauty. Muthesius praised examples of this

**Below:** Behrens, AEG Turbine Factory, Berlin, 1909. A modern Parthenon, complete with sculpture in the 'pediment' and columns (steel girders), using the language and monumentality of Ancient Greece to create a modern Temple of Industry.

**Right:** Taut, Glass Pavilion, Werkbund Exhibition, Cologne, West Germany, 1914. Designed to display the potential of glass, it was crowned with a prismatic dome composed of diamond panes, giving the dome its pointed shape.

style in the new building types of his time, such as railroad stations, bridges and steamships. He referred specifically to buildings that use the new materials, such as the Crystal Palace in London, the Bibliothèque Ste Geneviève and the Eiffel Tower in Paris, as examples of an architecture appropriate for the twentieth century. Another key figure in the development of the new aesthetic was Friedrich Naumann, a socialist politician with strong ideas on the social importance of art and architecture. Like Muthesius he encouraged the use of new materials and building types as representative of a new style which, for him, symbolized the power of industry and socialism to break the traditional power structure of politics. It was under the inspiration of Muthesius and Naumann that the cult of the machine was transformed into a reality.

### THE DEUTSCHER WERKBUND AND GERMAN ARCHITECTURE

The link between the socialist principles of the Arts and Crafts movement in England and the development of industrial design in practice was forged in Germany with the founding of the Deutscher Werkbund in 1907 by Hermann Muthesius, Karl Schmidt and Friedrich Naumann, the key event in the development of the modern movement. All three founders had strong views on the importance of industrial design. Schmidt was a cabinetmaker, who had founded the Deutsche Werkstätten für Handwerkskunst (German workshop for craftsmanship) at Hellerau in 1898. He encouraged the manufacture of well-designed and cheap machine-made furniture and the group exhibited examples of such furniture, designed by Schmidt's brother-in-law, Richard Riemerschmid, at an exhibition of industrial art in Dresden (1905-6). Between 1900 and 1907 a number of major architects were appointed to head various schools of arts and crafts in Germany. Muthesius was responsible for many of these appointments through his position as Superintendent of the Prussian Board of Trade for Schools of Arts and Crafts. It was part of a conscious effort at reform and the architects appointed were mainly designers who had rejected Art Nouveau, and many were linked with Olbrich's circle in Darmstadt. In 1902 van der Velde was appointed to head the Weimar school. The following year Behrens, who had been employed by Olbrich in Darmstadt since 1893, moved to head the Düsseldorf school and Poelzig was promoted from Professor of Architecture, to Director, at Breslau.

The role of Naumann, a socialist politician, in the foundation of the Deutscher Werkbund was critical. The importance of socialist principles to the development of the modern movement cannot be understated. Like its predecessors in the field of artistic reform, the group was opposed to eclecticism and, significantly, it deliberately chose to include industrial design as a form of art. The crucial characteristic of good design, according to the Deutscher Werkbund, was quality. This could be achieved either by hand or machine. In the inaugural speech of the Deutscher Werkbund, it was pointed out that lack of quality in industrial design was the result of the inability to use the machine, not any inferiority inherent in the machine itself. The foundation of the Deutscher Werkbund led to the formation of similar groups in other countries, notably Austria (1910) and Switzerland (1913). In England, the Design and Industries Association was founded in 1915.

The founding of the Deutscher Werkbund symbolized the growing emphasis on the functional and was supported by the new industrial patrons who showed a surprising readiness to accept the untraditional design concepts. In 1907 the managing director of AEG, Paul Jordan, arranged for the appointment of Behrens as architect and artistic adviser to the company. His duties included not only the design of factories, showrooms and workshops, but also the design of pieces of electrical equipment, such as radiators, lamps and kettles. He was also responsible for the design of the firm's publicity material, including writing-paper, posters and publications. This was an important post in the history of design, showing a desire on the part of AEG, to emulate their aristocratic contemporaries (and predecessors) such as the Grand Dukes of Hesse and Saxe-Weimar. Industrial wealth had begun to replace traditional patronage. The style of Behrens' work was very simple, showing a marked lack of ornament and an emphasis on functionality. In many ways the designs are similar to those of the Arts and Crafts designers in England but with one crucial difference: they were designed to be made by machine and not by hand. In this they represent the total rejection of one of Morris' most fervent beliefs.

Behrens' Turbine Factory for AEG, Berlin (1909) shows a major advance in the design of industrial building. He emphasizes the importance of the structure with the exposed metal frame and heavy concrete corner piers. The interior of the building is functional, as one would expect, but the exterior makes a more definite statement about the role of AEG in German society through strong visual links with the classical temple. The Small Motors Factory for AEG, Berlin (1910), used brick rather than concrete for the piers that support the roof, but both buildings suggest the curved forms of his earlier designs.

In his nonindustrial commissions, Behrens was far less innovatory. He replaced the romantic style of Darmstadt with a more austere approach to design, but still showed his preference for classical forms. The Art Building for the exhibition at Oldenburg (1905) shows the replacement of curved shapes, so prevalent at Darmstadt, with straight lines, both in structure and decoration. The cubic character of this pavilion was also apparent in his early houses, such as the Schröder House, Eppenhausen (1908-10). The severity of its form is emphasized by the use of quarry-faced masonry below with rough-cast walls above. The two-story apsidal portico in the center shows his reliance on classical tradition. His design for the German Embassy at St Petersburg, now Leningrad (1911-12) bears some relation to the Small Motors Factory, but German prestige dictated that plain brick piers should be replaced here with Doric columns. Behrens was the leading architect of his generation in Germany and his offices attracted a lot of talent. Three of the greatest twentieth-century architects, Gropius, Mies van der Rohe and Le Corbusier, all worked with Behrens during their formative years, and his combination of classicism and frank structural expression was to be of great significance in the development of their architecture.

**Below:** Mies van der Rohe, project for the Kröller-Müller Villa, The Hague, 1912. The colonnade and the suggestion of a projecting cornice on the right-hand block give this project a strong neoclassical flavor, appropriate to its function as an art gallery.

CHEIDT

Poelzig, appointed by Muthesius to head the Breslau Arts and Crafts School, was also involved in the design of the new industrial architecture. After World War I he became the principal exponent of German Expressionist architecture. His prewar buildings reflect this trend in his preference for curvilinear forms and contrasts in form and texture, in comparison to the classical austerity of Behrens and the other Werkbund architects. His Office Building at Breslau (1911) has bands of masonry, which separate the tiers of windows and curve around the corners of the building. In the Chemical Factory at Luban (1911-12), Poelzig used the contrast of curved and rectangular windows, spacing them in an unusual way, which reflected the stepped roofline and also the patterned brickwork.

Another figure whose major works belong to the postwar period was Bruno Taut. His two pavilions for the Steel Industry (Leipzig Exhibition, 1913) and the Glass Industry (Cologne

**Left:** Gropius & Meyer, Fagus Factory, Alfeld-an-der-Leine, West Germany, 1911. Elegant and modern: the steel-and-glass structure rests on a traditional brick podium.

**Below:** Gropius & Meyer, Fagus Factory, Alfeld-an-der-Leine, West Germany, 1911. Recessed supporting piers allowed the designers to wrap a glass curtain wall round the sharp corners, conveying weightlessness, in strong contrast to Behrens' AEG Turbine Factory.

Exhibition, 1914) deliberately exploit the structural potential of their respective materials rather than conforming to a functional reality. The 'Monument to Steel' consisted of stepped octagonal sections surmounted by a huge sphere whose diameter corresponded to the highest of the octagons. The style of Taut's glass pavilion developed out of his experiments with the material rather than traditional forms. The pavilion was constructed entirely in 'new' materials, with a concrete foundation and the circular base to the dome constructed with steel and glass 'bricks' as infill. The inscription around the dome (perhaps the only traditional element in the building) praises glass, contrasting it with brick which Taut considered an inferior material.

Mies van der Rohe worked in Behrens' office from 1908 to 1911 and the influence of Behrens can be seen in the neoclassical severity that characterizes all his buildings. His architectural style is probably the furthest from that of Poelzig, whose heavy and massive forms contrast with the delicacy and balance of Mies. Mies' early training had been as a decorative artist, and from 1905 to 1907 he worked as an apprentice to a furniture designer. One of his first independent projects after leaving Behrens' office was the Kröller-Müller Villa in The Hague (1912), designed to house the Kröller-Müller art collection, but never built. The projected plan shows many neoclassical elements inspired by the great nineteenth-century German neoclassicist, Schinkel. Mies had supervised the construction of the German Embassy in St Petersburg, Behrens' most strictly neoclassical building. Although the Kröller-Müller Villa shows a purer and more modern outline, this project, like the Embassy, is very much in the nineteenth-century tradition of a classical style appropriate for major government buildings and cultural institutions.

Walter Gropius, the son of a Berlin architect, had an architectural training, unlike many of his contemporaries, notably Mies van der Rohe. After graduating from Munich in 1905 he traveled in Spain, Italy and Holland before going to work in Behrens' office in Berlin from 1907 to 1910. In 1910 he wrote a pamphlet for AEG on the standardization of mass-produced houses, their aesthetics and their financing. This pamphlet is one of the first attempts to combine low-cost housing with good design. Previous efforts at large-scale housing in England, where good design had been a major issue, had been restricted to the wealthier

**Below:** Behrens, Kettles designed for AEG, c 1908-10. Behrens' designs were characterized by a lack of ornament and an insistence on functionality.

**Left:** Gropius & Meyer, Werkbund Factory, Werkbund Exhibition, Cologne, West Germany, 1914. Again dispensing with corner piers, the symmetrical façade is flanked by clear glass towers, housing the staircases

middle classes. Gropius wanted to do the same for workers' housing schemes. He criticized the individualism of such schemes as Bedford Park, near London, believing strongly in the industrial ethic of standardization. He also criticized English low-cost back-to-back terraced housing on the grounds that, although it achieved the aim of standardization, it was constructed for purely commercial, capitalist reasons and bore no relation to the comfort of the inhabitants. In this Gropius went beyond the paternalistic social reforms of such people as William Morris and Ebenezer Howard.

Like many architects of his generation, Gropius' designs went far beyond the traditional boundaries of architecture and included such diverse items as wall fabrics and a diesel locomotive. In 1911 he went into partnership with another protégé of Behrens, Adolf Meyer. Their first building was the Fagus shoe-last factory at Alfeld-an-der-Leine (1911), a major landmark in architectural history. There is no hint of ornament, no suggestion of a curve and no effort to convey monumentality. The design of the steel, glass and brick workshop block reduces the structure to its basic necessities, reflecting the function of the building and aims at a deliberately industrial aesthetic in preference to interpretations of more traditional forms and decoration, as in Behrens' Turbine Factory. The building shows the influence of functional factory construction in America and it is no coincidence that the patron of the project, Karl Benscheidt, was rebuilding his factory to incorporate improvements in industrial planning developed in America.

In 1914 the Deutscher Werkbund gave its first exhibition in Cologne. The exhibition included work by most of the Werkbund architects and provided a forum for much discussion on the opposing directions contained within the movement. The period 1900-14 was one of experimentation by individuals to find their own stylistic solutions to the problems they faced. They were united in a common cause and experienced the same desire to promote a new style based on an industrial and socialist ethic, not bound by the traditions of older architecture. This was comparatively easy in the field of industrial and commercial architecture, where patrons saw themselves as pioneers in a new area of power and were keen to construct new images for their achievements. In the more traditional architectural arena of public and domestic building these same architects responded in a more conservative manner, creating images for their patrons which owe more to nineteenth-century classicism than to the new industrial ethic.

The vast range of styles within the Werkbund shows the enormous variety of solutions open to them and it was hardly surprising, given the personalities involved, that power struggles arose to establish leadership. The inevitable conflict between the superiority of man-made or machine-made art, between individualism and standardization, between creativity and conformity and between traditionalism and modernity came to a head in 1914. In the debate that followed, Muthesius argued for standardization and the introduction of a universal aesthetic and van der Velde argued for the individuality, creativity and independent genius of the artist. Muthesius won the argument and the stage was set for the modern movement.

MERCURY

# 2/ARCHITECTURE BETWEEN THE WARS

Graham, Anderson, Probst & White, Wrigley Building, Chicago, Illinois, 1924.

World War I had a devastating effect on Europe and its repercussions were felt worldwide, both in a change in the balance of power and the massive economic depression of the early 1930s. The Treaty of Versailles, which had been drawn up with the aim of punishing Germany and her allies, attempted to avoid a repetition of the war by restricting the size of Germany's army, forbidding her to manufacture armaments and by breaking up the old dynasties of the prewar era into a series of smaller and new states based on racial groups within the old empires, such as Czechoslovakia, Austria, Hungary and Romania. Germany was contracted, losing land to Poland and France and colonial possessions in Africa to Britain and France. By far the most crucial aspect of the Treaty was the demand for enormous reparations to be paid by Germany to the Allies, and the country was thus given little opportunity to recover economically. Disastrous inflation followed and the US dollar, which had been worth 4 German marks before the war, was worth 192 marks in January 1922 and 4,200,000,000 marks by November 1923.

The United States was relatively unaffected by the war. The poor economic state of postwar Europe, the diffusion of political power and the chaotic effects of the Russian Revolution gave America a position of far greater economic and political importance than it had previously possessed. The expansion of the American economy was dramatic, unfettered by the traditional European dislike of materialism. As President Coolidge remarked, 'The business of America is business.' In 1920 there were 9,000,000 cars in the United States, by 1930 the figure had soared to 30,000,000. The Wall Street Crash of 1929 was a disaster but its effects were worldwide and the United States retained her economic supremacy.

The atmosphere of social reform that had characterized the prewar period continued in a spirit of expediency with the continuing extension of political enfranchisement from the privileged to the masses. However, the Russian revolution in 1917 was greeted with wholehearted terror of a similar overthrow of traditionally established authority in the rest of the industrialized world. Major steps were taken to control communist and socialist tendencies. The repression of left-wing ideas in Germany was sparked off by the Communist, or Spartacist Revolt in 1919. Antisocialist fervor led to the nationalist Fascist march on Rome, headed by Mussolini in 1922. In Germany an anticommunist movement was set up by the heavy industry leaders in 1919, making big financial contributions to nationalist parties and thus sewing the seeds of the next war.

The association in the minds of those with political power between a growing laxity in social morals and the threat of a communist revolution led to Prohibition in America (1919) and the banning of the full text of D H Lawrence's *Lady Chatterley's Lover* in England (1928). By 1933 the pragmatic approach to progressive ideas which characterized the interwar years, had been replaced in Germany and Russia by a dictatorial clamping down on the freedom of expression, enforced on the population by Hitler and Stalin. It is no coincidence that Germany and Russia were two of the main focal points for innovations in architectural thought and design during the early part of this century. The rise to power of Stalin, during the late 1920s, and Hitler in 1933, led to the expulsion or repression of progressive thinkers in all fields of the arts and sciences.

Artistic and architectural thought of the period 1919 to 1939 was initially imbued with a fervent left-wing idealism, which faded toward 1930 through disillusionment with reactionary governments. This is mirrored in the enormous stylistic gap between the buildings and designs of the *avant-garde* and the commissions of conformist society in general. The theoretical ideas of Muthesius and the Deutscher Werkbund, which had advocated standardization of design were developed in the interwar years in an attempt to consolidate viewpoints and to develop an international style.

The interwar years were a period of discontent and disturbance, in part due to the disastrous economic effects of the peace treaties concluded at the end of World War I, but also because of a rising tide of nationalism. The unprecedented depression sparked off by the Wall Street Crash of 1929, exacerbated by the deflationary measures used to combat it, led to the breakdown of democracy in a number of countries, including Poland and Germany, and the establishment of totalitarian rule under Stalin. In Britain, hunger marchers filled the streets and riots broke out between Fascist and Communist supporters.

By 1933 the West was beginning to reemerge from the Great Depression with a changed political face. The totalitarian régimes of Stalin, Hitler and Mussolini had begun to recover themselves sufficiently from a economic point of view to consider their next objective: territorial aggrandizement. For Hitler, this meant rearmament, in contravention of the Treaty of Versailles, and his invasions of Czechoslovakia, Austria and finally Poland led directly to the outbreak of World War II.

Up to 1933 the German cities of Berlin and Munich had been the cultural centers of Europe. Apart from literature, theater and the arts in general, Germany had also provided the focal point of the *avant-garde* movement in architecture. However, the International Style developed by Gropius and his colleagues at the Bauhaus was essentially cosmopolitan in outlook and this found expression in the formation of the *Congrès Internationaux d'Architecture Moderne*, or CIAM in 1928. One of its most important precepts was the recognition of the developing role of the State in architectural patronage and that architects no longer belonged to an artistic élite but were directly involved in political issues. CIAM was to be of major significance, particularly after the pan-German government of the National Socialists closed the Bauhaus in 1933, forcing the German architects of the International Style to emigrate.

Hitler's policies against political activists, especially against radicals and Jews, led to the emigration of many of the leaders of the artistic and intellectual life in Germany, including the writers Bertholt Brecht and Thomas Mann, the scientists Albert Einstein and Sigmund Freud and art historians such as Ernst Gombrich and Niklaus Pevsner. After 1933 Paris took over as the center of Europe's *avant-garde* in literature and painting. In architecture, the focus of the modern movement moved, with its protagonists, to the US, where it has, so far, remained.

## NEW IDEAS: CONSTRUCTIVISM AND DE STIJL

The success of the Russian Revolution had a tremendous impact on artistic thought. The complete overthrow of an established ruling power encouraged a similar rejection of traditional rules in art, and the new authorities encouraged this repudiation of bourgeois, capitalist attitudes to culture. Indeed, there was a conscious rejection of all traditional elements in art on a scale unimaginable in the West. Innovation in Russia was inspired by prewar developments, particularly Cubism and Futurism, and Russian artists and designers began to blur the boundaries between the traditionally distinct areas of painting, sculpture and architecture. They put their talents into the creation of revolutionary propaganda through the Proletkult (Organization for Proletarian Culture, founded by Bogdanov after the first, abortive revolution of 1905) which was in charge of spreading the revolutionary message in visual terms to a population with a high proportion of illiteracy. Architectural ideas remained theoretical due to the combined effects of the war and the economic blockade of Russia by the West not lifted until 1922.

Three schools of art were founded around 1920 which acted as the centers for the development of new ideas. In 1919 the painter Malevich founded Unovis (the School of New Art) in Vitebsk and in 1920, two art schools were founded in Moscow, Inhuk (the Institute for Artistic Culture) and Vkhutemas (Higher Artistic and Technical Studios). Expanding Cubist and Futurist ideas, these schools abandoned formal representationalism in art for abstract design. Malevich's classic painting, *The Black Square* (1913-15), literally a black square on a white background, was intended to convey emotional sensation. His later works further exploited abstract rhythms using color and basic geometrical forms – circle, square and diagonal – to convey movement, weight and depth. His interest in architecture was developed in a series of three-dimensional experiments with ideas from his paintings showing an asymmetrical and dynamic grouping of masses, the 'Architectons.' Another artist, Lissitzky, started his 'Proun' experiments in 1919 under Malevich with planes and masses grouped along diagonals in dynamic compositions.

Meanwhile, in Moscow two schools of thought were developing at Inhuk. Malevich and Kandinsky, the first president of Inhuk,

**Below:** Melnikov, USSR Pavilion, Exposition des Arts Décoratifs, Paris, France, 1925. One of the few practical examples of Russian Constructivist theories, with intersecting masses composed to emphasize the diagonal.

believed that the artist was only concerned with abstract design and not with its practical and utilitarian application. Art was separate from industrial design. This view was opposed by Tatlin, Rodchenko and others (often called the Productivists), who believed that the artist had to become an engineer and to use his energies and talent to benefit society in a practical and direct way. Not surprisingly, the role of the machine as a liberator of man from labor was crucial. Tatlin's activities included the design of a stove which produced more heat for less fuel (1918-19) and he produced paper patterns for making functional clothing. His attitude to design united the demands of the Russian population, experiencing one of the worst winters for years, with the desire to see the formerly élitist artist participating in real social problems.

Tatlin's architectural projects used modern materials and, for the first time, experimented with their potential quite unhampered by traditional concepts of style. His Monument to the Third International (1919-20) consisted of two intertwining spirals of steel, reaching a height of over 1000 feet, enclosing congress rooms shaped as a cube, a pyramid and a cylinder, all designed to rotate at different speeds. Its abstract form was designed to convey the spirit of the Revolution, the dynamic spiral breaking out from the masses. In comparison to the Eiffel Tower it exhibited a radically different style, where dynamism and technical extravagance replaced the static and monumental.

The conflict between the artists, like Malevich and Kandinsky, and the Productivists reached a peak in 1920 and Kandinsky's program for teaching at Inhuk was rejected. Over the next few years it became serious enough for the artists to leave Moscow. Malevich returned to Vitebsk, but some of the others went to Germany and France, Kandinsky ending up on the permanent staff of the Bauhaus.

Constructivism developed out of the ideas of Tatlin and Rodchenko and it was worked out as a system at Inhuk in 1921. Closely connected with communist ideology, it rejected all exclusivity and bourgeois status, emphasizing the practical and utilitarian aspects of design. At Vkhutemas a debate began among the Constructivists about the degree to which utilitarianism should govern teaching. Ladovsky and his colleague, Lissitzky, encouraged their students to explore their imaginations, ignore technical limitations and to examine fully the relationships between space and form, so developing the idea at an intellectual level before putting it into practice. It was this aspect of postrevolutionary Russian thought that was to be so influential through Lissitzky's later work in Europe.

One of the few buildings to express modern Russian theories in practice was Melnikov's USSR Pavilion for the Paris Exhibition (1925). The diagonal, so important in the conceptual projects of Malevich, Tatlin and Lissitzky, appears in the form of a staircase. This staircase, decorated with diagonally placed girders, reminiscent of a row of raised swords, intersects both the ground plan and the body of the building, questioning traditional concepts of interior and exterior space. As rebuilding slowly got under way again in the 1920s to cope with rapid industrialization, Russian architects were faced with practical problems. The lack of funds and the urgency of the situation led to pragmatic and functional solutions which reflected the needs of the state rather than the experiments of the earlier idealists. This pattern reflects the way in which the idealism of the Revolution faded during the 1920s after the death of Lenin. With Stalin's rise to power Russian architecture retreated into the safety of historicism.

Whereas Constructivism was born out of revolution, De Stijl was the result of Dutch neutrality during World War I, allowing artists to

**Left:** Tatlin, Monument to the Third International, 1919-20 (model). Abstraction in architecture; an imaginative design that could not be built. This steel structure, over 1000 feet high, was to enclose congress halls and offices, and was painted red in memory of the Revolution.

**Below:** Rietveld, Red-Blue chair, 1917. Design reduced to its basic structural elements and composed entirely of straight lines, painted in primary colors. De Stijl insisted on an intellectual approach to design and rejected ornamentation.

continue the development of prewar ideas while artistic life in the rest of Europe largely stood still. In 1917 a magazine started in Leiden called *De Stijl*, based on the theories of a painter, Theo van Doesburg, and its contributors included other painters such as Piet Mondrian and architects, notably J J Oud, Robert van t'Hoff and Gerrit Rietveld. The first manifesto of the group (1917) recognized that war was destroying the old world and that the machine was crucial to the genesis of the new. De Stijl's attitude to the machine was far closer to the practical approach of the Deutscher Werkbund than to the romantic idealism of the Futurists. Developing ideas current in prewar Europe, they eschewed ornament, praised straight lines and experimented with the basic elements of spatial construction. Mondrian, like Malevich, was influenced by the abstract experiments of the Cubists. During the early years of the war he worked with van Doesburg, gradually evolving a purely abstract style using horizontal and vertical lines and the three primary colors with white, black and grey as contrasting tones. Using only basic elements, they rejected all other shapes and colors as impure. Whereas Malevich's use of the diagonal gave his designs an inherent dynamism, van Doesburg and Mondrian developed a static style.

In applying these concepts to architecture, the members of De Stijl were much influenced by Wright's early experiments in spatial construction (published 1910-11) and by Berlage's use of brickwork and insistence on structural honesty. Following Mondrian and van Doesburg's experiments on paper, the predominant form was the straight line rather than the curve. The use of the cube, an expression of mass, was rejected in favor of intersecting planes so that the walls created a relationship between exterior and interior space. The basic colors of De Stijl painting were also incorporated into its architecture, not as decoration but rather as a means to define space.

Van t'Hoff had visited Chicago before the war and his direct experience of Wright's work led to his villa at Huis ter Heide, Utrecht (1916), with its flat projecting roof and heavy horizontal emphasis. Although it predates the formation of the group, many of the ideas associated with De Stijl are present in its simplicity, developing interest in the exploitation of planar

**Below:** Rietveld, Schröder House, Utrecht, the Netherlands, 1924. An imaginative patron allowed Rietveld to experiment with spatial construction, creating an abstract house, composed of interpenetrating planes, to diffuse the traditional distinction between exterior and interior space.

**Left:** Oud, Hook of Holland estate, the Netherlands, 1924. Oud's mature style developed from De Stijl in response to the practical demands of designing low-cost housing estates, using concrete construction and thin metal windows.

surfaces. Initially denied patronage, the first true De Stijl works were on a small scale. Rietveld's Red-Blue chair (1917) shows a traditional structure but reduced to its minimum elements. It was followed by other pieces of furniture, such as his sideboard (1919) which develops the theme of interpenetrating planes. His first major architectural commission came from a designer, who appreciated his modern style. The Schröder House, Utrecht (1924) destroys the basic cube by the use of a series of interlocking planes of wall, supported with thin metal strips painted in the De Stijl colors, red, blue and yellow. It shows a greater delicacy than van t'Hoff's house at Huis ter Heide and it is considerably more abstract. The plan of the upper floor reflects this abstraction by breaking down traditional wall divisions between rooms and using movable partitions. The lack of definition between exterior and interior that results from the interpenetrating structure shows how far De Stijl architects had developed Wright's ideas.

Oud's early projects show the influence of the vernacular style of Berlage. The Villa de Vonck, Noordwijkerhout (1917) is built of brick with a pitched gabled roof but the interior, the result of a collaboration between Oud and van Doesburg, shows a definite break with tradition, its clear white walls contrasting with the rectilinear pattern of De Stijl colors on the floor. In 1918 Oud was appointed chief architect to the city of Rotterdam. Faced with a severe housing shortage and a lack of funds, his De Stijl theories were put into practice with austere and rectilinear designs, such as the Taanderstraat block, Tusschendijken estate, Rotterdam (1920). By 1924 he had broken away from the mainstream of De Stijl, and the Hook of Holland estate (1924) shows his style in a mature form. The importance of this estate lies in the uniformity and the simplicity of the design. It is built of concrete and the plain treatment of the surfaces owes much to the non-decorative teachings of De Stijl, although the curved walls at the corners show a concern for mass quite unlike the elementarist elegance of Rietveld. The harmony that Oud achieved in this project was to be of great importance for the development of the International Style.

**Below:** Oud, De Unie Café, Rotterdam, the Netherlands, 1925. An architectural version of a De Stijl painting, composed of horizontal and vertical lines.

**Above:** Taut, design from *Alpine Architektur*, 1919. Pure fantasy, these mountain temples reflect the escapism of postwar Expressionist design.

The year 1921 marked the beginning of a new phase in De Stijl. After the lifting of the Western embargo on trade with Russia, Lissitzky was sent by Vkhutemas to Europe with the specific task of contacting the European *avant-garde* movements. Together with a number of Russian émigré artists, including Kandinsky, Lissitzky brought Russian theories to Europe. His influence on De Stijl was enormous. Van Doesburg abandoned his purist compositions with their horizontals and verticals in favor of the Russian diagonal. In 1923 van Doesburg and van Eesteren held an exhibition in Paris which included a design for the interior of a university hall, with rectangular shapes set at angles on the walls, creating a more dynamic effect than earlier De Stijl works, and he used a similar effect in the Café L'Aubette, Strasbourg (1928-9). Lissitzky's influence was also apparent in other areas. His 'Proun' experiments were the basis for a series of axonometric, quasi-architectural projects by van Eesteren and van Doesburg exploring the variety of interlocking surfaces, dating from around 1923.

The importance of Constructivism and De Stijl lies in the development of intellectual design. The idea of experimentation with abstract forms, not bound by traditional notions of architectural design, nor by practical considerations, was taken up by the modern movement creating a new kind of architect with an intellectual, almost mystical status quite different from the mundane and practical architect of tradition.

## POSTWAR GERMANY: EXPRESSIONISM AND THE BAUHAUS

Expressionism was not a coherent movement like Constructivism or De Stijl, neither is it a very satisfactory category for grouping a number of visually distinct buildings and designs, but it provides an umbrella for works created in the aftermath of a war, which destroyed the hopes of prewar society. In the despair and disorganization that characterized postwar Germany, Expressionist architecture appears as a reaction to the efficient industrial style of the Deutscher Werkbund. Expressionist architecture developed in this context before the war, for example in van der Velde's Werkbund Theater for the Cologne Exhibition (1914). It was utopian, idealized and appealed more to the senses than to the intellect in its search for an appropriate style to express the new order.

In 1918 Taut organized the Workers' Council for Art, which, as its name suggests, was linked to the radical socialist movement in postwar Germany. The group was disbanded after the Spartacist Revolt in 1919, but its members, who included Taut, Gropius and Mendelsohn, continued their association through a series of letters called 'The Glass Chain.' Under the direction of Taut, this became the main forum for Expressionist ideas in Germany. In 1919 Taut published *Alpine Architektur*, which included utterly fantastic designs for temples on top of mountains. They were to be built of steel and glass as a comment on the ugliness of the brick and stone cities below. After the horrors of war, their utopian and unreal quality was understandably escapist. In 1921 Taut was appointed architect to the city of Magdeburg where he was faced with the postwar reality of lack of funds and a severe housing shortage. His austere housing estates were enlivened by brightly painted public buildings and kiosks to display advertising slogans.

A similar problem faced the Dutch authorities who appointed Oud in Rotterdam and commissioned Michel de Klerk and Piet Kramer to design badly needed housing projects in Amsterdam. De Klerk and Kramer's designs show an expressionist style with more coherence than the general European movement. It coexisted with De Stijl and like De Stijl, drew inspiration from the brick architecture of Berlage. De Klerk's work on the Eigen Haard estate (1913-20) showed how effectively brick could be used to enliven cheap housing. His later buildings developed the use of curved bricks to create light and cheerful architecture without the heaviness associated with German Expressionism. Kramer's work is very similar to de Klerk's, particularly his use of brick and curved corner features. Their buildings in Amsterdam established a tradition of well-designed low-cost housing in Holland which inspired later generations of architects to similar success in public building.

Brick was also used by Behrens and Mies van der Rohe in their postwar architecture. Like many of the Deutscher Werkbund architects, their postwar designs had a strong Expressionist feel to them. Behrens' I G Farben complex at Höchst (1920-4), for a company that had made large profits out of the war through the production of toxic gases, was not restricted by lack of funds. The same restless effect as Poelzig achieved in his theaters with applied decoration was obtained by Behrens in the variety of shapes and shades of brickwork. Mies van der Rohe's monument to the leaders of the Spartacist Revolt (1926) used a variety of brick surfaces composed in an abstract block.

Ironically, the greatest Expressionist works in Germany were created not by Taut, but by Poelzig and Mendelsohn. Poelzig's Grosse Schauspielhaus, Berlin (1919), was a theater built for the impresario Max Reinhardt. Significantly, he was not restricted by the lack of funds that Taut faced in Magdeburg. The interior was decorated with stalactites, hanging from every available surface, a total fantasy. He

**Below:** De Klerk, Eigen Haard housing estate, Amsterdam, the Netherlands, 1913-20. Good design, simplicity and imagination were the hallmarks of cheap housing in Holland after the war.

**Above:** Poelzig, Das Grosse Schauspielhaus, Berlin, 1919. Another escapist fantasy, but designed deliberately as an appropriate style for a place of entertainment.

**Right:** Gropius, Bauhaus complex, Dessau, East Germany, 1925-6. The complex involved a variety of activities, with offices, workshops, classrooms, library and accommodation for students and staff, combined in a cohesive whole, revolutionary in its insistence on functionality and lack of ornament.

managed a similar effect in his project for the Festspielhaus, Salzburg (1920). Mendelsohn's Einstein Tower, Potsdam (1919-22) is the complete antithesis of prewar rational architecture. Its organic form, in curves of concrete and plaster, disguises the brick structure beneath and shows an imagination unrestrained by the authoritarianism of the International Style.

It is quite a surprise that Gropius, the archpriest of the modern movement, should have gone through an Expressionist phase after the war. His War Memorial at Weimar (1922), a jagged and aggressively austere work, bears testimony to this and to his despair at the destruction of the prewar ideals of developing a modern style. Gropius had been appointed as head of the Weimar School of Art in 1915, after van der Velde's resignation. In 1919 he reopened it under the new name of *Das Staatliche Bauhaus*. His manifesto (1919) declared that the school aimed to educate students for a new community of artist-craftsmen, undivided by traditional class distinctions between artist and craftsman and united by a common spirit to build, decorate and furnish buildings in the style of the future. This relates directly to the late-nineteenth-century efforts in Britain and Germany to bring art education out of its élitist academic cloister and into a more positive relationship with industry. The ideals of the Arts and Crafts movement were reflected in his choice of the name 'Bauhaus,' a recall of the *Bauhütte*, masons' lodges of the Middle Ages. Gropius envisaged a team of craftsmen educated to create cathedrals of the new age.

This process of education involved three stages. The first stage, a preliminary course, introduced by Johannes Itten and Georg Muche in 1921, aimed to clear the apprentice's mind of artistic preconceptions and to introduce him to the principles of creativity, fulfilling the dual function of indoctrination of Bauhaus ideals and assessment of individual abilities. At the second stage the apprentice learned a craft such as metalwork, weaving or pottery and finally he took a course on industrial design. Expressionist painters and designers formed the bulk of the original staff at the Bauhaus and therefore it was inevitably associated with left-wing ideas, which caused problems in the highly unstable atmosphere of postwar Germany. Gropius and his staff managed to survive the attacks made on them largely as a result of the resolute attitude of the Ministry of Culture in Weimar.

By 1924 the Bauhaus had developed away

from Expressionism toward a more functional approach to design. The lack of objectivity inherent in Expressionism, and the escapist notions of Itten, led to conflict between the practical aims of Gropius' original manifesto and the direction taken by the Bauhaus in the first years. This change of approach was encouraged by the appointment of van Doesburg (1921) and Kandinsky, the erstwhile head of Inhuk (1922). Itten resigned in 1923 and was replaced by László Moholy-Nagy, a Hungarian lawyer who had been influenced by Lissitzky in Berlin. Gropius began experimenting with form under the influence of van Doesburg and in 1923 he published plans for standardized housing units. Their rational and objective quality indicated the direction in which the Bauhaus was to develop.

After 1924, the Bauhaus became closely associated with the *Neue Sachlichkeit*, or New Objectivity, initially the reaction of artists to Expressionism, characterized by an unemotional attitude to design, functionalism and overt commitment to the ideals of socialism. This was reflected in the appointment of Hannes Meyer (1927) to head the architecture department. Meyer's early training and practice as an architect had been closely connected with the radically left-wing ABC group in Basle, committed to the New Objectivity.

In 1925 the Bauhaus moved from Weimar to Dessau. The new buildings for the school, designed by Gropius (1925-6), were the definitive expression of the Bauhaus style. The clean lines reflected Gropius and Meyer's prewar factories and the buildings showed little Expressionist feeling, but the complex developed the concept of functional design beyond industrial architecture. Like the factory complex that develops as its needs change, the highly organized plan was asymmetrical with carefully placed blocks suggesting this looser development, formality to express informality. Gropius' exploitation of industrial materials, concrete, glass, and steel marks an important achievement in architecture from a stylistic and a technical point of view. The curtain wall of the workshop block gives a lightness and simplicity to the structure which deliberately

**Above:** Mendelsohn, Einstein Tower, Potsdam, East Germany, 1919-22. Like Gaudí, Mendelsohn uses curved, organic forms, producing a building which departs from all traditional expectations of what a tower should look like.

**Right:** Gropius, Bauhaus workshop block, Dessau, East Germany, 1925-6. The lightness of the structure results from inset concrete piers, allowing glass to meet glass at the corners – functional design for the first time outside the realm of industry.

**Right:** Breuer, Bauhaus chair, 1926. Steel tubing and stretched fabric combined to create the ideal Bauhaus product: functional, machine-made and without unnecessary ornament.

**Far right:** Gropius, Siemensstadt estate, Berlin, 1930. Financed by the Siemens industry, this project was constructed from standardized units, the uniform individual apartments with modern conveniences.

contrasts with the relative heaviness of the concrete forms, and the aesthetic of the style is in its use of materials, not ornament. The buildings made a clear antihistorical and proindustrial statement about the activities that went on inside. The Bauhaus was not only responsible for the creation of a radically new architectural style but also for major developments in the design of furniture and other aspects of interior decoration. One of the school's first pupils, Marcel Breuer, was put in charge of the furniture workshop (1926). His rational approach to design, his emphasis on the use of pure geometric forms, such as the cube or the cylinder, together with the use of materials such as glass and steel, shows in his Bauhaus chair, first produced in 1926 and copied ever since.

In 1928 Gropius resigned from the Bauhaus to pursue private practice and he was succeeded by Hannes Meyer. Under Meyer's influence, the Bauhaus moved much closer to the socialism of the New Objectivity and he developed a more socially responsible program, designing and producing simple and cheap items with the emphasis on social rather than

20

aesthetic criteria. Meyer's left-wing politics led to a campaign against him by the right wing and he was forced to resign in 1930, moving to Moscow. The appointment of Mies van der Rohe as his successor did little to change the situation and the Bauhaus was closed by Hitler in 1933.

### THE INTERNATIONAL STYLE

The term 'International Style' was first used by Hitchcock and Johnson as the title to the catalogue of the first International Exhibition of Modern Architecture, held at the Museum of Modern Art, New York in 1932. They saw the style developing during the early years of the century in, for example, Loos' Steiner House, Vienna (1910) and the works of Oud and Rietveld in Holland. Gropius, Mies van der Rohe and Le Corbusier all made their own crucial contributions to the development of the International Style. One of the main reasons for its impact was the highly articulate and persuasive literature of Le Corbusier, Gropius and others. The other major figure of twentieth-century architecture, Frank Lloyd Wright, remained outside the movement, even though his early works were seminal to the development of the International Style. In 1932 the movement was still essentially European, only moving to the US after Hitler's rise to power.

In 1929 Taut summarized the main characteristics of the new style in his book *Modern Architecture*. Buildings were designed to fulfill a functional need, and beauty was inherent in successful functional design. A building that worked well was beautiful, one that did not was ugly. Repetition was encouraged, as a means of expressing identical needs – a far cry from the individualism of Expressionism.

After leaving the Bauhaus in 1928, Gropius was mainly involved with the design of low-cost housing estates in Dessau and Berlin, beginning with the Törten estate, Dessau (1926-8). This was a series of two-storied terraced blocks arranged in concentric rings around a four-story block of flats and a co-operative building. The houses were all identical and furnished with custom-built items from the Bauhaus workshop. The Dammerstock estate, Karlsruhe (1927), shows a more varied approach with two-story houses and six-story blocks of flats. The living accommodation was more interesting in layout and shows how Gropius was trying to improve the aesthetic quality of workers' housing. This estate coincided with a pamphlet 'How can we build cheaper, better, more attractive houses?' in which Gropius considered the roles of the three key people involved in low-cost housing. The architect's task was to interpret the sociological needs of the inhabitants into designs. The engineer's

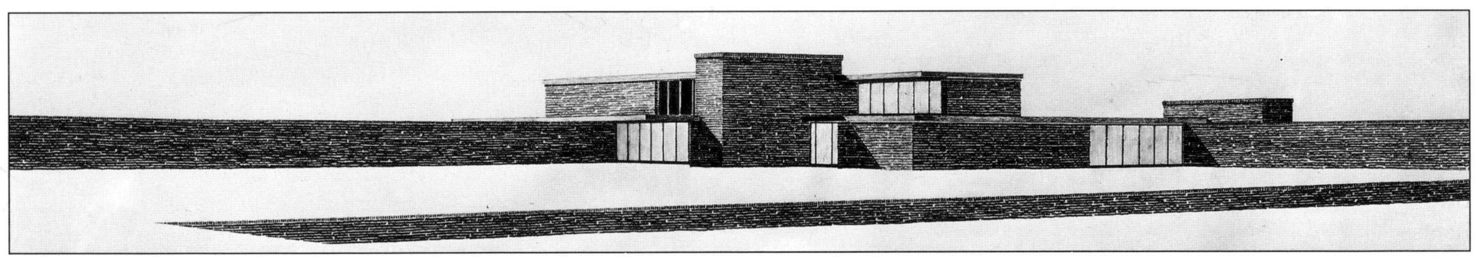

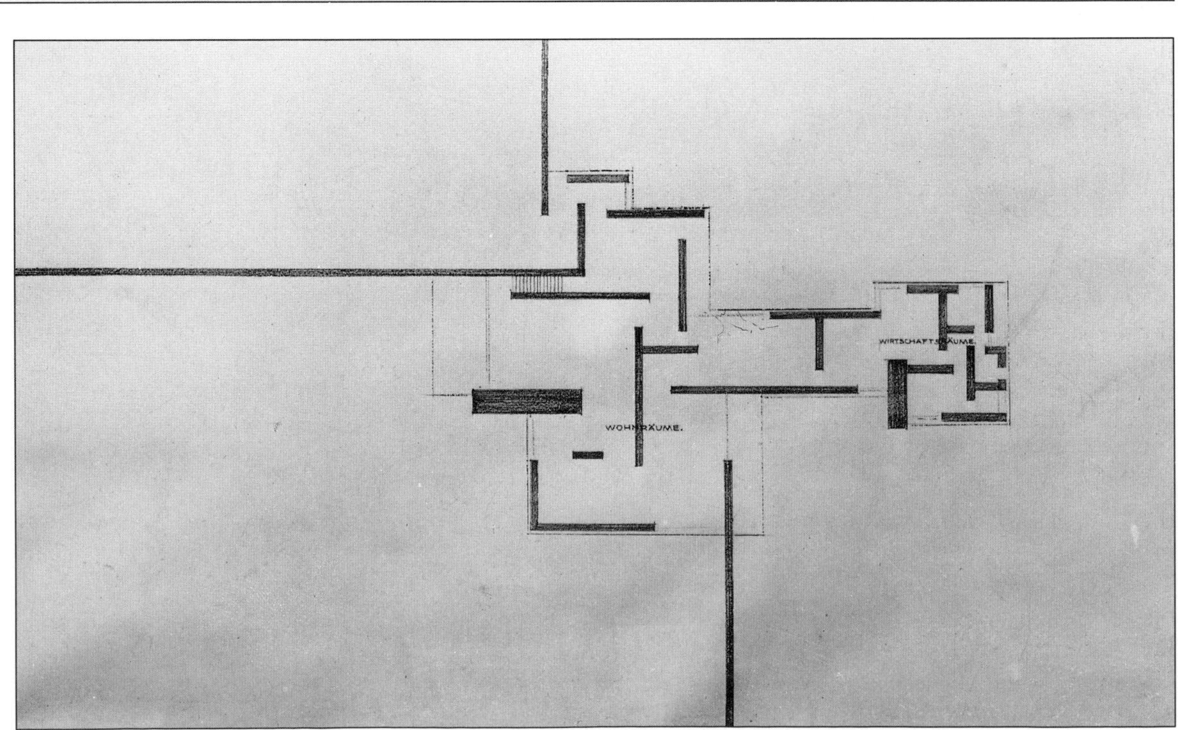

**Above and right:** Mies van der Rohe, project for a brick country house, 1922. Art or Architecture? This shows Mies' informal approach to interior space.

task was to develop new construction methods and to design standard items such as windows and doors. The financier's job was to find the funds for building and for the manufacture of the standardized units. The Siemensstadt estate, Berlin (1930), financed by the Siemens industry, shows the success of Gropius' ideas in developing the factory aesthetic.

Mies van der Rohe's architectural style is distinct from that of Gropius, although it belongs to the same tradition. His training in Behrens' office and his postwar Expressionism follow a similar pattern to Gropius but his early concern for the neoclassical, apparent in his design for the Kröller House, sets them apart. After the war Mies, like so many of his contemporaries; abandoned Expressionism in favor of a more rational approach. In 1923 he contributed to the first edition of a magazine, *G* (for *Gestaltung*, or creation), edited by Lissitzky, and through his contact with Lissitzky he developed his interest in spatial construction.

In 1927 the Deutscher Werkbund held their first major exhibition since Cologne (1914) on the Weissenhof estate in Stuttgart with the aim of illustrating the topical problem of housing. This exhibition was the first to show the white, cubic and flat-roofed housing that became known as the International Style. Mies was in charge of the layout of the projects by architects such as Oud, Le Corbusier, Gropius, Taut, Poelzig and Behrens, contributing a design of exceptional elegance himself. His comments on the problem of low-cost housing show his concern for spatial design. He considered the skeleton structure crucial to allow freedom in organizing internal space, with movable walls around a fixed core of bathroom and kitchen.

**Above:** Mies van der Rohe, German Pavilion, Barcelona Exhibition, Spain, 1929. Simplicity and elegance are the key elements in a style which Mies made so popular in the commercial atmosphere of postwar America.

**Left:** Mies van der Rohe, Barcelona Chair, 1929. Stylish and luxurious with leather upholstery: a chair designed for the executive, rather than Breuer's worker.

**Above:** Mies van der Rohe, Tugendhat House, Brno, Czechoslovakia, 1928-30. Movable screens in marble and ebony break down the traditional concept of the house as a series of rooms.

**Right:** Le Corbusier, Pavilion d'Esprit Nouveau, Paris Exhibition, France, 1925. A desire for standardization and quality in modern low-cost design led to this prototype of Le Corbusier's 'machine for living in.'

This concept of the flexible plan, seen in practice in his Weissenhof block, shows a concern for individual freedom missing in the authoritarian statements of Taut and Gropius.

Mies used this principle of flexible design in the German Pavilion for the Barcelona Exhibition (1929), dividing the interior asymmetrically with screens of marble and plate glass, opaque and clear. The building was constructed of steel, glass and marble and much of its beauty lies in Mies' positioning of these materials in a simple and infinitely elegant structure. Mies' Barcelona chair also belongs to this exhibition.

For the Tugendhat House, Brno, Czechoslovakia (1928-30) the wealth of his patron allowed Mies a far greater range of materials than low-cost housing ever could. The dining area was separated from the basic living area with a semicircular screen of macassar ebony and another screen of figured marble divided the remainder. Like his earlier buildings the house had a strong horizontal emphasis on the exterior, hugging the ground much as Wright's Robie House had done. Both these buildings exhibit the main characteristics of Mies' work, an informal approach to interior space, a love of rich materials and a simplicity of line.

Le Corbusier (born Charles Edouard Jeanneret) was a crucial figure in the development of the International Style. His background was eclectic. He had come into contact with the Arts and Crafts movement and Art Nouveau while a student. In 1907 he went to Vienna with the intention of working with Hoffmann, but changed his mind. He met Garnier that same year and was strongly influenced by his ideas on town-planning. In 1908 he worked with Perret in Paris, developing an interest in the potential of concrete, and in 1910 he studied industrial design in Behrens' office. He visited Turkey and Greece in 1911-12 and Ottoman architecture was a decisive influence. In 1917 he gave up his Swiss practice and moved to Paris where, through Perret, he met the painter Ozenfant.

In 1918 Ozenfant and Le Corbusier published *Après le Cubisme* attacking Cubism for having degenerated into mere decoration. They evolved their own purist interpretation of cubist ideas in *Le Purisme* (1920). Their paintings show an emphasis on form and a lack of decorative detail, inspired by the purity of machinery. The first of many architectural treatises by Le Corbusier, *Vers Une Architecture*, was published in 1923. It had already appeared

L'ESPRIT
NOUVEAU

in part in the magazine that Ozenfant and he had founded in 1920, *L'Esprit Nouveau*, and represented a deliberate attempt to mark the beginning of a new epoch: the machine age. Like Gropius and Taut, Le Corbusier was a passionate believer in standardization. The illustrations to *Vers Une Architecture* juxtapose images of past standardization, notably the Parthenon, with modern racing-cars, airplanes, factories and the grain silos of America. Mechanization had destroyed the culture of the past and new solutions had to be found through the machine, for the problems of the present. Governed by his theme of reducing everything to a human scale, the house was 'a machine for living in.'

His first project had been the Dom-Ino House (1914), a basic framework of six columns, two floor slabs and a flat roof of reinforced concrete. These basic units could be arranged into blocks and were to be produced on the assembly line. This project developed into the Citrohan House, first constructed for the Paris Exhibition (1925) as the Pavilion d'Esprit Nouveau, after the magazine. The term *Citrohan* was a deliberate play on words, recalling the giant French automobile manufacturer, Citroën, and suggesting the same standardization of production as the car. The house had notable features such as a living-room two stories high and a roof area which was treated as private outdoor space. His later houses developed the Citrohan style with simple rectilinear plans, large areas of windows and no ornament.

Le Corbusier was also concerned with town-planning and in 1922 he published a treatise on the subject, *Une Ville Contemporaine*. The scale of the project (3,000,000 inhabitants) sets him apart from his predecessors, Sant'Elia and Garnier. Whereas their projects were utopian, Le Corbusier attempted a more realistic proposal, accepting the capitalist system as the basis for the city. This was heavily criticized by the French Communist newspaper, *L'Humanité*. One of the important innovations of the project was an attempt at traffic classification. He recognized the different needs of the pedestrian, delivery vehicles, private car, and through traffic, and tried to rationalize their progress. Equally modern was his understanding of increasing density toward the center of a city, proposing 60-story office blocks for the business area. Like the garden city planners before him, Le Corbusier stressed the importance of greenery. The residential areas were designed with the ideas he had developed in the Citrohan housing projects. His theories were partially realized in housing developments at Pessac (1926) and Liège (1926). He also contributed plans for the redevelopment of city centers such as Paris (1925) and Moscow (1933).

The estate at Pessac, near Bordeaux, financed by a rich industrialist, Henri Frugès, consisted of 130 reinforced-concrete-frame houses, of varied design but all derived from the Citrohan type, illustrating his repeated efforts to introduce the standardized house and standardized house features. He appealed to industrialists in 1925 to produce standard window units, so that the architect could compose around them. Standardization, the essence of the machine ethic, was fundamental to the architects of the International Style, notably Le Corbusier, Gropius and Taut.

In 1926 Le Corbusier developed his 'Five Points of Architecture':

(1) *pilotis* raising the house from the ground – to introduce more light and to free the ground space for parking or a garden
(2) a roof garden for private exterior space
(3) the free plan, facilitated by the skeleton structure, allowing independent interior partitions
(4) ribbon windows to improve lighting
(5) the free façade, free in the structural sense from the basic skeleton.

These features occur, singly or together, in many of the private houses he designed including the La Roche-Jeanneret House, Auteuil (1924), Maison Cook, Boulogne-sur-Seine (1926), Villa Stein, Garches (1927) and the Villa Savoye, Poissy (1929-30). These houses were commissioned by patrons with strong artistic

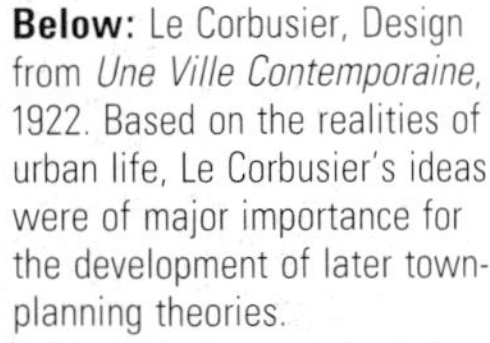

**Below:** Le Corbusier, Design from *Une Ville Contemporaine*, 1922. Based on the realities of urban life, Le Corbusier's ideas were of major importance for the development of later town-planning theories.

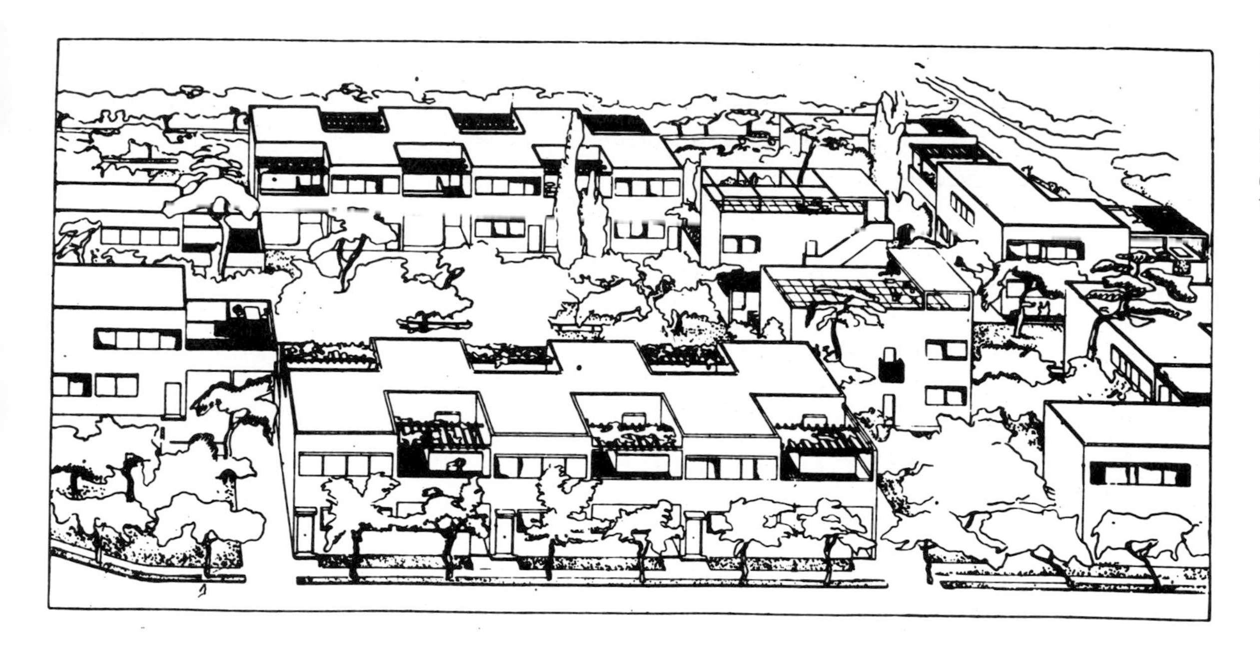

**Left:** Le Corbusier, Housing estate at Pessac, near Bordeaux, France, built 1926. A purist belief in standardization imposed uniformity on the occupier and ignored the need for personalization.

links, whose attitude to the modern movement was enlightened. William Cook was an American painter and Michael Stein, the brother of Gertrude Stein, was a collector of modern art. Far from being universally acceptable, the aesthetics of the International Style were limited in their appeal to the *avant-garde.*

The idea of an international style, transcending national boundaries, resulted in the collaboration of the talents of Le Corbusier, Gropius,

**Below:** Le Corbusier, Villa Savoye, Poissy, Seine-et-Oise, France, 1929-30. Stylish and not homely. An interior shot shows an interest in abstraction and the purity of line.

**Above:** Le Corbusier, Villa Savoye, Poissy, Seine-et-Oise, France, 1929-30. This was the image of modernity. Le Corbusier's clients were mainly middle-class intellectuals and artists.

**Right:** Shreve, Lamb & Harmon, Empire State Building, New York City, 1930-2. 102 stories high, this was a considerable structural achievement but it is often criticized for its lack of innovation in design.

**Far right:** Reinhard & Hofmeister, Rockefeller Center, New York City, 1932-9. The rigid New York zoning regulations led to a fashion for stepped-back skyscrapers, so unlike the rectangular glass boxes of postwar America.

and other architects in the formation of the *Congrès Internationaux d'Architecture Moderne,* or CIAM in 1928. This was an important development in the search for a new style for the twentieth century, in architecture.

## COMMERCE AND MODERNITY

The cult of the International Style successfully masks the bulk of architecture created between the wars, denigrating it as *petit-bourgeois* and commercial. But commercial it was, and unashamedly so, especially in America. The socialist principles and industrial style of Gropius, Taut, Le Corbusier and Mies van der Rohe had little appeal to the unrepentant capitalist. The view that industrial building was a lesser form of architecture persisted as did the idea that ornament, especially traditional ornament, was the distinguishing mark of more prestigious projects. This was anathema to the International Stylists, whose functionalism, lack of decoration and standardization was despised. Most of the architecture of the period developed along more traditionalist lines, slowly evolving styles which broke far less dramatically with the past.

New money imitated the old. In America, Gothic persisted as a style appropriate to the church, and Cram's Cathedral of St John the Divine, New York (1926) is typical in its insistence upon tradition. Collegiate Gothic continued to express the academic ideal, in fervent imitation of Oxford and Cambridge, with the

Harkness Memorial Tower and Quadrangle at Yale (1917), the Memorial Church at Harvard (1929-33) and countless other schools and colleges across the country. Classical styles retained their popularity for the new patrons of cultural institutions. Financed by the railroad magnate, the Henry E Huntingdon Art Gallery Library, Los Angeles (1925), has paired Ionic columns in the best Renaissance tradition and, as late as 1937, John Russell Pope used classical ornament on the National Gallery of Art, Washington DC. Kahn, whose industrial buildings were innovatory in their functionality and exploitation of new materials, used a classical design for the William L Clements Library, University of Michigan, Ann Arbor (1920-1). Typical of the establishment, Kahn disapproved of the International Style, making a clear stylistic distinction between industrial design and 'proper' architecture.

The design of a skyscraper, essentially a commercial building, involved the provision of enough accessible office space to make the venture commercially viable. The ultimate expression of this was the Empire State Building, New York (1930-2), the tallest building in the world from 1932 to 1971, with 102 stories. As competition for land in Manhattan increased, zoning laws were introduced in New York (1916) to allow for light at street level by requiring stories above a certain height to be set back from the edge of the lot. The rules also allowed for a quarter of that lot to be built on without height restrictions. This had an important stylistic

**Right:** Graham, Anderson, Probst & White, Wrigley Building, Chicago, Illinois, 1924. A proud image for commerce: grand and pinnacled, with an emphasis on mass, not height.

**Left:** Hood & Howells, Chicago Tribune Tower, Chicago, Illinois, 1922. This Gothic skyscraper, complete with flying buttresses and pinnacles, won the 1922 competition against entries by designers like Gropius, and shows a strong preference for traditional styles for the commercial image.

impact, resulting in stepped profiles, sometimes surmounted with a tall tower on the unrestricted quarter.

Sullivan's developments at the end of the nineteenth century toward an appropriately functional design for the skyscraper were to some extent ignored. The American economy expanded during the 1920s and the architectural symbol of this wealth, the skyscraper, aspired to the status of prestigious architecture, adopting the style and decoration of more traditional building types. Gilbert's Woolworth Building, New York (1913), suggested the trend of postwar skyscrapers in its choice of Gothic as the decorative sheathing over the modern construction. In addition to its traditional status, the vertical emphasis of Gothic made it the perfect historical style for expressing the verticality of the skyscraper.

The 1922 Chicago Tribune Tower competition attracted 259 entries from all over the world. The winning entry was chosen by a

**Above:** Halliday & Agate with G G Scott, Battersea Power Station, London, England, 1929-54. Now one of London's protected landmarks, the grandeur of the four chimneys illustrates the importance that was attached to the generation of power.

panel of Chicago politicians, journalists and one architect, representing popular American taste. Designed by Hood and Howells, it continued the Gothic precedent of the Woolworth Building with a four-story base and a soaring central section crowned by a small tower, apparently supported by flying buttresses.

Second place went to a design by Eliel Saarinen, whose stepped form was emphasized by a strong verticality. It was medieval in inspiration in contrast to the overtly applied Gothic ornament of Hood and Howells' winning design. Designs by Gropius & Meyer and Taut were also rejected, both aggressively angular and devoid of ornament in the best Bauhaus tradition.

Hood's later skyscrapers are plainer and lack historical detail. The Daily News Building, New York (1930), continues the vertical emphasis of the Gothic skyscrapers, but the McGraw-Hill Building, New York (1932) experiments with a horizontal effect using a series of superimposed cubes. It earned Hood an entry in Hitchcock and Johnson's exhibition of the International Style and praise for its 'lack of applied verticalism.' The other American skyscraper in the exhibition was Howe and Lescaze's Philadelphia Savings Fund Society (PSFS) Building, Philadelphia (1931-2), which returned to Sullivan's intention of expressing the various interior functions on the exterior, with visually distinct blocks to represent the different functions of the various parts of the building and thus initiating the custom of housing lifts and services in a separate amenities block. Going beyond Sullivan, this attention to function resulted in asymmetrical structures. Like Kahn and others, Howe's innovations were restricted to commercial buildings. He was a prolific designer of neomedieval suburban houses, notably one for the president of the PSFS, J M Willcox, who clearly recognized a distinction between the private image and the commercial one. Other commercial buildings expressed their aspiring status in the choice of classical ornament, such as Morris' Cunard Building, New York (1921), Lutyens' Midland Bank, London (1924-39) or Bosworth's American Telephone and Telegraph Building, New York (1923), which experimented with Doric and Ionic to differentiate the functions of the various levels. The extension to Liberty's, London (1924), revived Elizabethan forms. Baroque, a sumptuous interpretation of classical designs, was particularly popular for hotels.

The new style of the 1920s and 1930s was the Moderne, characterized by two distinct phases, Art Deco and a more streamlined version which followed in America in the 1930s. Art Deco was popularized at the Exposition des Arts Décoratifs, Paris 1925, ironically also the site for the début of the International Style with Le Corbusier's Pavilion d'Esprit Nouveau and Melnikov's USSR Pavilion. Developing out of Expressionism, Art Deco responded to the popular appeal of the exotic in non-European civilizations like China and Egypt (Tutankhamun's tomb was discovered in 1922), and the primitive cultures of South America. Like Art Nouveau, it was an attempt to create a modern style less dependent on traditional historical forms and found expression in commercial architecture, notably department stores, offices and hotels.

Highly stylish, Art Deco was characterized by a lavish use of colorful and extravagant materials, such as the black and gold of Hood's American Radiator Building, New York (1924) and Morgan, Walls and Clements' Richfield Building, Los Angeles (1928-9; now destroyed), the chrome and black glass of Ellis and Clarke's Daily Express Building, London (1931) or the aluminum spire of Van Alen's Chrysler Building, New York (1926-30) – an elegant skyscraper which epitomizes the style with its finely detailed but simplified ornament and its glittering peak. Moderne rather than modern. The use of light was an important feature of Art Deco. Only the rich could afford electricity during the late nineteenth century but as demand rose during the 1920s it became cheap enough to be widely available. Its decorative potential was exploited by commerce as a symbol of modernity, for example the neon-lighted clock on Beelman's Eastern Columbia Building, Los Angeles (1929), or combined with mirrors in Bernard's Strand Palace Hotel foyer, London (1929). Electricity also lit up the

**Above:** Van Alen, Chrysler Building, New York City, 1926-30. The elegance of the aluminum spire adds style to an otherwise plain building and typifies Art Deco.

**Left:** Van Alen, Chrysler Building, New York City, 1926-30. The elevator door is an example of the elaborate interior, which exudes wealth with expensive materials and Moderne design.

**Far left:** Milne, Claridges extension, London, England, 1930. Art Deco was popular as a modern image of glamor, in preference to the austerity of the modern movement.

RADIO CITY
MUSIC HALL
RADIO CITY
THE GREAT CHRISTMAS SHOW WITH "PETE'S DRAGON"
RADIO CITY
MUSIC HALL
TOW AWAY ZONE

façade of Urban's Reinhardt Theater, New York (1928), emphasizing its role as a palace of the night.

Art Deco was used extensively in the architecture of entertainment such as Morgan, Walls and Clements' Warner Brothers Western Theater (now the Wiltern Theater) Los Angeles (1930-1), and its extravagance was most fully developed in the interior decoration of cinemas and ballrooms. Lavish and sumptuous, they are often criticized for a lack of subtlety, but who wanted subtlety? The cinema and the ballroom were for entertainment, a chance to escape from drab reality into the fantastic. Like Poelzig's Grosses Schauspielhaus, the theaters of Hollywood exploited the exotic with Egyptian and Chinese in Grauman's Theaters by Meyer and Holler (1922 and 1927). Roxy's Radio City Music Hall (1932) was decorated in opulent materials, including a gilded ceiling, black glass, mirrors and polished metal to reflect light. Trent and Lewis' New Victoria Theater, London (1930), imitated Poelzig more directly with shell forms suspended from the ceiling to diffuse the lighting. The variations are endless but the intention to provide a dramatic and escapist setting for entertainment remained the same.

With the worldwide Depression sparked off by the Wall Street Crash of 1929, the decorative excesses of Art Deco were replaced by a much plainer, streamlined version of the style. Inspired by the machine ethic of the International Style, Streamline Moderne imitated the more functional forms of the ship and airplane with its curves, porthole windows and metal strips emphasizing horizontality. The Depression affected the building industry and the style found its greatest outlet in consumer goods and the New York World's Fair (1939).

## THE IMAGE OF THE STATE

State architecture is state propaganda. The choice of style, whether conformist or reactionary, historical or modern, makes an important statement about the ideology of the political régime that commissioned it. The inspiration of Greece and Rome for the political reforms of the nineteenth century was expressed visually in the predominant use of classical imagery for government buildings. Classical architecture can be used to convey many political images, democratic or imperial, moral or extravagant. Above all it conveys an image of power and tradition, making it an ideal choice for the expression of establishment, either real or aspiring. The preference for classical as the appropriate style for state architecture persisted well into the twentieth century, despite the dissatisfaction with nineteenth-century eclecticism and the development of new nonhistorical styles, such as Art Nouveau, Art Deco and the International Style. However, the developing taste for simplicity and lack of ornamentation

**Above:** Brown Derby Café, 3377 Wilshire Boulevard, Los Angeles, California, 1926. The simple, modern and easily recognizable image of a hat to convey style and class.

**Left:** Radio City Music Hall, Rockefeller Center, New York City, 1932. The austerity of the exterior does not aim to prepare us for the extravagance of the interior.

**Right:** Radio City Music Hall, Rockefeller Center, New York City, 1932. Even the Ladies' Powder Room enters into the spirit of escapism, creating a cocoon of luxury and extravagance.

**Below:** Meyer & Holler, Grauman's Theater, Hollywood, California, 1927. The Chinese pagoda, a vision of Oriental delights and an ideal image for the entertainment industry.

**Below right:** Gilbert, Supreme Court, Washington DC, 1935. Classical styles continued to be used for state architecture throughout the twentieth century, the ideal image to convey morality, tradition and establishment.

affected its interpretation and a simplified classicism was used, for example, by Behrens in his German Embassy, St Petersburg (1911-12). After World War I this simplified classicism was developed in an attempt to create a more fitting style for the new century. Political establishments in countries such as Britain and America distrusted modern ideas and the rise of socialism, but the reactionary régimes in Italy, Russia and Germany were openly hostile. Their rejection of the International Style and its socialist connotations was hardly surprising, nor was

**Above:** Wallis Gilbert & Partners, Hoover Building, Perivale, Middlesex, England, 1932-5. A simplified neoclassical structure with Art Deco decoration.

their steadfast reliance on tradition in their architecture.

In Scandinavia simplified classicism developed as a reaction to National Romantic architecture of the late nineteenth century, with such buildings as the Faaborg Museum, Copenhagen (1912), by Carl Petersen, and the Police Headquarters, Copenhagen (1918-22), by Hack Kampmann, and spread from Denmark to Sweden and Finland after the war. Asplund's Central Library, Stockholm (1920-8), shows the reduction of a classical structure to unadorned simplicity. In Finland, where the incentive to create an image for the newly independent state was more urgent, simplified classicism represents a more obvious rejection of the past. In 1904 Saarinen had designed Helsinki's railroad station in a simplified way, influenced by developments at Darmstadt, but it was not until after the war, and Finnish independence from Czarist Russia, that this degree of simplification could be used for government buildings. Sirén's Parliament Building, Helsinki (1926-31) symbolizes this achievement.

In America nineteenth-century neoclassical architecture did not represent outmoded tradition of prewar Europe nor a political past best forgotten. On the contrary, it symbolized America's independence and present power. This was reflected in the persistence of traditional forms of classicism in Washington DC with the Lincoln Memorial by Bacon (1912-22) and the Jefferson Memorial by Pope, Eggers and Higgins (1934-43). The Jefferson Memorial is based on the Pantheon, with its domed

rotunda and pedimented portico, but the circular body is open and colonnaded very much in the image of the dome of the Capitol. The image of the Capitol had formed the basis for earlier state capitols, but this began to change. Goodhue's design for Nebraska State Capitol, Lincoln, Nebraska (1922-32), shows the influence of simpler forms. The central domed rotunda was replaced by an immense tower crowned by a small dome, based on the classical, but considerably simplified, and the decoration shows the influence of Art Deco. The simplified classicism of Cret's Hartford County Building, Hartford, Connecticut (1926), is more typical, lacking the commercial references of Art Deco.

In England the style developed rapidly. Lutyens was commissioned to design a number of war memorials, including the Thiepval Arch, Belgium (1919) and the Cenotaph, London (1919-20). The choice of the arch and the cenotaph to commemorate both the triumph and the dead shows reliance on the classical tradition, but they are treated with exceptional austerity verging on the Expressionist. This simplified classicism was developed in city halls throughout England, such as Vincent Harris' Sheffield City Hall (1920-34) and his extension to Manchester Town Hall (1927-30), or James and Pierce's Norwich City Hall (1932-8), which shows the influence of Scandinavian architecture. The style was also used in academic institutions, where its classical origins made it an appropriate choice, such as Wornum's Royal Institute of British Architects Building, London (1935), Scott's New Bodleian Library, Oxford (1935), and Holden's Senate House for London University (1933-7). It found more positive expression in the conscious exercises in public image such as Lutyens' and Baker's designs for the new imperial capital at New Delhi, India (1912-31) and the competition in 1927 for the League of Nations Building, Geneva. After World War I the League of Nations was founded in the cause of peace and such an innovatory institution might have been expected to break new stylistic ground, but although the competition attracted entries from architects like Le Corbusier, the committee opted for traditional but simplified classicism to express its image.

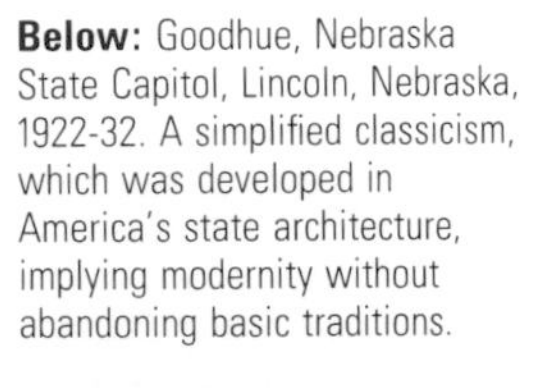

**Below:** Goodhue, Nebraska State Capitol, Lincoln, Nebraska, 1922-32. A simplified classicism, which was developed in America's state architecture, implying modernity without abandoning basic traditions.

**Left:** Nénot et al, League of Nations Building, Geneva, Switzerland, 1927. Unsure of its political role, the League of Nations commissioned a building which tried to sit in both modern and traditional camps.

In Russia, Stalin's rise to power saw the beginning of a repressive régime, the end of intellectual Constructivist theory and the victory of tradition. In 1931 a competition was held to design the Palace of the Soviets, Moscow. Like the League of Nations Building competition, this attracted many entries, including designs from Le Corbusier, Gropius, Mendelsohn, Poelzig, and Perret, as well as Russian architects. The judges (chaired by Molotov, a close associate of Stalin) chose a conservative and classical design by Iofan which was developed over the next few years, in collaboration with other architects, into a monumental and austere structure with stepped circular colonnaded sections surmounted by a statue of Lenin. The discussion in the Russian press on the issue of the choice of an appropriate design illustrates the importance of style for the image of the state. Public opinion was in favor of a neoclassical design, but there were serious problems in finding a historical style that

**Left:** Shchukov & Gelfreikh, Lenin State Library, Moscow, 1928-40. The traditional features of this building are in marked contrast to the genuine innovations of Constructivist architecture and show how reactionary Russia became after Lenin's death.

accorded with communist ideals of freedom; Gothic had religious overtones, Romanesque was too feudal and Italian Renaissance was too aristocratic. The choice of democratic Ancient Greece was criticized because the society had been based on slavery. Ironically the building, started in 1937, was never finished and ended up in the 1960s as a giant open-air swimming pool. The rejection of the designs of the modern movement was significant. They were essentially idealized images of a progressive, socialist and industrialist culture, inappropriate to the repressive nature of Stalin's régime. The modern style was criticized in the press for its derivation from the machine, the tool of capitalist slavery, and it was thus itself considered capitalist. The extent to which Russian architecture had changed is illustrated in a comparison of the Russian Pavilions at the Paris Exhibitions of 1925 and 1937. By 1937 the innovations of Melnikov's 1925 Pavilion had been replaced by a building of austere and monumental classicism, appropriately placed opposite Speer's German Pavilion. One of Stalin's major innovations was the Moscow Metro (begun 1934) with a series of underground station interiors of powerful and awe-inspiring classical monumentality.

In Germany the International Style was the open expression of all Hitler despised. One of his first acts as Chancellor was the closing of the Bauhaus in 1933. He then embarked on a policy of building housing in a traditional indigenous style, with pitched roofs and gables, deliberately replacing the apartment blocks of the International Style with estates of individual houses. This suggests an awareness of the

**Above:** Komsomolskaya station on the Moscow Metro, c1938. A Baroque extravaganza and a long way from the intellectual rigor of Constructivist design.

**Far left:** Lutyens, Viceroy's House, New Delhi, India, 1920-31. The visual symbol of the jewel in Britain's Imperial crown, Lutyens' design combined all the grandeur of Ancient Rome, with little reference to Indian tradition.

**Left:** Troost, The Brown House, Munich, West Germany, 1936. The Nazis totally rejected the modern movement and looked to older traditions, such as Renaissance Rome, for the design of their architecture.

**Right:** Mies van der Rohe, project for the Reichsbank, Berlin, 1933. This modern design for the state bank did not appeal to Hitler's Third Reich.

social problems inherent in faceless blocks, but the reasoning was more overtly political; to diffuse potential strongholds of opposition. The state image of the Third Reich was powerfully neoclassical, austere and simplified, with the images of the state – the swastika and the eagle – dominating the structures in good imperial tradition. Hitler appointed Speer as state archi-

**Below:** Speer, Zeppelinfeld Stadium, Nuremburg, West Germany, 1936. Speer designed architecture to impress, drawing directly on the image of Imperial Rome.

tect in 1934 and he drew up plans for a new Berlin, imitating the monumentality of ancient Rome with a triumphal avenue, 130 yards wide, and many severely neoclassical buildings of which the Domed Hall of the Reich was the most impressive, with paired Doric columns, a huge domed rotunda and a long, stepped approach. The sheer scale of Nazi architecture sets it apart from the smaller building of the rest of European simplified classicism, showing an obvious desire to impress.

In Italy the position was different. Mussolini came to power in 1922, before the development of the modern movement in Italy, which began effectively in 1926 with the founding of 'Gruppo 7' in Milan. The group's early works show the influence of Russian Constructivists and Le Corbusier, for example in Giuseppe Terragni's apartment block, Novocum, Como (1928-9). By 1931 the familiar debate between traditional and modern had spilled into the political arena, but the solution in Italy was different. The government-backed union of architects condemned both the eclecticism of traditional style and the antihistorical stance of the modern, suggesting that the image for Mussolini's Italy should not ignore the glories of the past but develop a new interpretation. The degree of tolerance shown by the authorities to modern styles is evident in the number of buildings constructed between 1922 and 1939. Trucco's Fiat Factory outside Turin (1923) included an automobile testing track on the roof; a major landmark in the use of concrete. Nervi's experiments with concrete exploited its potential and dictated his style in a manner comparable with Perret and Le Corbusier, notably his Stadio Comunale, Florence (1930-2) and aircraft hangars at Orvieto, Orbetello and Torre del Lago (1936-41).

Mussolini, in direct emulation of his illustrious predecessor the Emperor Augustus, concentrated his architectural energies on the restoration of his capital city to its former grandeur, with town-planning projects and buildings, such as the new university and the Foro Mussolini (now the Foro Italico), a vast sports complex to the north of Rome. His most drastic project was the reorganization of the Borgo between the Vatican and the Tiber, opening up a wide, ceremonial approach to St Peter's and destroying many of the narrow streets and palaces of Renaissance Rome. He also commissioned a new monumental center for Rome, initially intended as the center for an exhibition planned for 1942, the Esposizione Universale di Roma (EUR). The plan for EUR was drawn up by a group of architects, including Giuseppe Pagano and Marcello Piacentini, both of whom had been involved in the new

**Below:** Nervi, Military aircraft hangar at Orbetello, Italy, 1936. Nervi's experiments with prefabricated concrete make him one of the most exciting designers of the century.

**Above:** Terragni, Casa del Fascio (del Popolo), Como, Italy, 1932-6. Italian Rationalist architects based their modern designs on strict geometrical rules and deliberately chose not to make a complete break with tradition.

university and town-planning projects in central Rome. The complex of buildings, outranking anything achieved by Hitler or Stalin, are stark and severe simplifications of their classical prototypes, compromising between the rationalism of the modern movement and the monumentality of Italian and Roman achievements of the past.

The return to classical imagery in Russia and its reinterpretation in Germany and Italy reflect the return to traditional authoritarian political systems in all three countries. The Brazilian experience was very different. In 1930 the Vargas Revolution saw the final overthrow of imperial Portuguese rule and its replacement by a government under the leadership of Vargas, committed to industrialization and social reform. Architects like Lúcio Costa had been influenced by European developments through the writings of Le Corbusier, but the International Style had been unpopular with the establishment, firmly rooted in European tradition. By appointing Costa as head of the school of Fine Arts, the new régime adopted an antihistorical and overtly modern style as the visual expression of their break with the past. In 1935 a competition was held for designing the Ministry of Education and Health building. Through the far-sighted intervention of the Minister of Education, Gustavo Capanema, Costa was appointed to head the team of architects, which included Oscar Niemeyer and Affonso Eduardo Reidy. In 1936 Le Corbusier was invited to Brazil to act as consultant on the project and his three-week stay firmly established the modern movement in Brazil. Between 1937 and 1943 many impressive buildings were designed in Brazil, based initially on the ideas of Le Corbusier but rapidly developing into a mature and independent style.

## THE SPREAD OF THE INTERNATIONAL STYLE

Although initially disliked, the ideals of the International Style slowly began to permeate the architectural establishment, initially through the prolific writings of Le Corbusier and Gropius and the Bauhaus publications of Kandinsky, Moholy-Nagy, Oud, van Doesburg and others, and later through the International Style exhibition held in New York (1932). The final spur was mass emigration from Hitler's Germany.

An Austrian émigré, Richard Neutra, had an important effect on the spread of the style in California. Neutra, who arrived in America in 1923, had been strongly influenced by Loos. He had worked with Wright in Chicago and initially his designs owed much to Wright's ideas, but he kept in touch with European developments through magazines and texts, and it was these ideas which dictated his own style. His

**Above:** Costa, Niemeyer et al, with Le Corbusier, Ministry of Education and Health, Rio de Janeiro, Brazil, 1936-8. A modern image for a new state dedicated to social reform. Brazilian architecture soon moved away from Le Corbusier and developed its own local traditions.

major project was the Lovell Health House, Los Angeles (1927-9), commissioned by Dr Lovell, who had shown considerable interest in new ideas. Constructed on a prefabricated steel-skeleton frame with extensive glazing, it shows a knowledge of the form and materials of the International Style well in advance of other American architects of the period.

A few European architects developed along similar lines, discarding the simplified classicism of the period in favor of the innovations of the modern movement, notably in Scandinavia. Asplund's classicism, evident in his Stockholm Library (1920-8), is missing in his designs for the Stockholm Exhibition (1930), which are constructed entirely of steel and glass. In Fin-

**Left:** Neutra, Lovell Health House, Los Angeles, California, 1927-9. One of the few buildings that experimented with the International Style in the United States, before the war.

land the same pattern showed in the works of Alvar Aalto and Erik Bryggman. Their designs for the Jubilee Exhibition at Turku (1929) show the influence of Le Corbusier. Aalto's Tuberculosis Sanatorium, Paimio (1929-33) was hailed as an architectural landmark, on a par with the Dessau Bauhaus. Function was the basis of its design, a collaboration between Aalto and the doctors, with maximum attention paid to the patients' needs. The same functional approach was used in his library complex, Viipuri (1927-35), where the undulating ceiling of the lecture hall was designed to improve acoustics.

In England, the critic Clive Bell had declared his allegiance to the machine age as early as 1914, but little progress was made. Experiments with modern materials continued with Owen Williams' Boots Factory, Beeston (1930-2) – which is still one of the world's largest reinforced-concrete buildings – and his Empire Pool, Wembley, London (1934) with its large concrete cantilevered roof, but the style was slow to develop in traditional building types. Le Corbusier's *Vers Une Architecture* was translated into English in 1927 and some buildings influenced by Le Corbusier appeared soon after, notably Emberton's Royal Corinthian Yacht Club, Burnham-on-Crouch (1930), built on piles out into the sea with a façade which was constructed almost entirely of windows, and Connell's Ashmole House, Amersham, Bucks (1930). Built for Bernard Ashmole, head of the British School in Rome, this was almost pure Le Corbusier, with its flat roofs, strip windows and white cubic form. Structurally, however, it lacked the purity of a Corbusier house with its Y-shaped plan which stemmed from a hexagonal core.

The exhibition of the International Style, held at the Museum of Modern Art, New York in 1932, marks the beginning of the spread of the style from its narrow confines in Germany, Holland and France to worldwide importance. Although the bulk of the projects in the exhibition were by architects associated with the Bauhaus – such as Gropius, Le Corbusier, Mies van der Rohe, Breuer, Oud and Mendelsohn – Hitchcock and Johnson, the organizers, also included projects by other architects, such as Aalto, Asplund, Bryggman, Emberton, Neutra, and two skyscrapers: Hood's McGraw-Hill Building and Howe & Lescaze's Philadelphia Savings Fund Society Building. Hitchcock and Johnson's definition of the International Style involved three principles: skeleton structure, standardization and lack of ornament. The skeleton structure removed the necessity for load-bearing walls, allowing architecture to be concerned with volume rather than mass, or to use Hitchcock and Johnson's simile, an 'open box' rather than a 'dense brick.' Standardization combined the irregular functions of individual parts of a building into a regular whole, and the absence of ornament avoided any historical association.

Ironically, it was Hitler who inadvertently was responsible for the spread of the International Style. His antisocialist and anti-Semitic campaigns, starting with the closing of the Bauhaus in 1933, led to the emigration of all the major German architects. Some initially came to Britain, such as Breuer (1933-7), Gropius (1934-7), and Mendelsohn (1934-41), all of whom finally settled in the United States; others went there directly, like Albers (1933), Moholy-Nagy (1937) and Mies van der Rohe (1937). Hannes Meyer went to Russia.

The arrival of Gropius, Breuer and Mendelsohn in Britain was preceded by that of Berthold Lubetkin, a Russian who had been studying with Perret in Paris and been influenced by Le Corbusier. The appearance of these architects in Britain at a time of heavy investment in the building industry and growing recognition of their innovations on the part of the *avant-garde* gave a major stimulus to the expansion of the International Style. The Bauhaus émigrés all went into partnerships with British-based architects, Gropius with Maxwell Fry, Mendelsohn with the naturalized Russian Chermayeff, and Breuer with the author of *The Modern House*, F R S Yorke. Lubetkin arrived in London in 1930 and started work with five recent graduates of the Architectural Association under the name of Tecton. One of their first commissions was the Penguin Pool, Regent's Park Zoo, London (1933), where their original use of concrete was displayed for animal rather than human habitation. Their Highpoint estate, Highgate, London (1933-8), two blocks of luxury apartments, followed Le Corbusier in the use of *pilotis* and was visually innovatory although, with its load-bearing walls, structurally less so.

Patronage of the International Style in Britain came largely from the cultured and progressive upper middle classes, very much on the pattern Le Corbusier had experienced, and unlike that of Gropius in Germany. Most of the commissions were in the *avant-garde* centers of Cambridge and London (Hampstead and Chelsea), and the patrons ranged from the artist Augustus John to the intellectual Julian Huxley. Connell continued his innovatory work for Ashmole with a house in Hampstead for a solicitor, Geoffrey Walford, at 66 Frognal (1938) in partnership with Lucas and Ward. Gropius and Fry designed 66, Old Church Street, Chelsea (1935-6) for the playwright Benn Levy and his wife, the actress Constance Cummings. Mendelsohn and Chermayeff designed 64, Old Church Street, Chelsea (1935-6) for the Cohen family. Through their links in Cambridge, Gropius and Fry also obtained the commission for Impington Village College, outside Cambridge (1936), but the committee choosing a design for

**Right:** Aalto, Sanatorium, Paimio, Finland, 1929-33. The functional design of this building shows how Aalto absorbed the theories of the modern movement.

**Above:** Lubetkin & Tecton, Penguin Pool, Regent's Park Zoo, London, England, 1933. This piece of abstract concrete sculpture, influenced by Constructivist ideas, provides the penguins with Art.

an extension at Christ's College, Cambridge, were not persuaded by the pro-Gropius faction and this ultimately led to his departure for the United States and Harvard. The left-wing climate of Cambridge in the 1930s made it an important British center for the development of the International Style, with works by Raymond McGrath, George Checkley and H C Hughes.

Mendelsohn and Chermayeff's major commission was the De La Warr Pavilion, Bexhill-on-Sea (1934), for the mayor of the town, Earl De La Warr, who was also the chairman of the National Labour Party. Unlike most of the other projects, which were largely private houses for the middle classes, this was a project with some of the socialist idealism of the Bauhaus, a pleasure palace for working-class entertainment, with a cinema, cafeteria, bars, dance floor, swimming-pool and offices. The design takes the differing functions of the parts of the building into account, with an enclosed box housing the cinema at one end and the eating/drinking areas at the other overlooking the sea. In the British context it is strikingly modern, demonstrating Mendelsohn's ability to use steel, glass and concrete in an expressive way.

Le Corbusier's practice in France suffered as a result of the economic depression of the 1930s, and he concentrated on theoretical works. However, his contacts elsewhere were crucial for the spread of the International Style. Through CIAM he influenced the Spanish architect, José Luis Sert, collaborating with him on a residential project in Barcelona (1933). Sert designed the Spanish Pavilion for the Paris World's Fair (1937), which was dominated by the neoclassical German and Russian Pavilions of Speer and Iofan. Sert's Pavilion was one of the few designed in the International Style and was the site of the first showing of Picasso's masterpiece on the Spanish Civil War, *Guernica*. Le Corbusier's influence in South America has already been mentioned and he was also in contact with a group of South African architects, under the leadership of Rex Martienssen. Le Corbusier's ideas, together with the writings of Gropius and other Bauhaus figures, also had an important influence in Japan and two architects, Kunio Mayekawa and Junzo Sakakura, came to Europe to work with Le Corbusier. The influence of modern European ideas was clear in Sakakura's Japanese Pavilion for the Paris Exhibition (1937), where traditional wooden structural techniques were replaced by a steel frame, the simplicity of Japanese style lending itself easily to modern movement ideals.

The Bauhaus émigrés who ended up in the United States were welcomed into American academic institutions with open arms. Never was a battle so easily won. Albers started teach-

**Above:** Mendelsohn & Chermayeff, De La Warr Pavilion, Bexhill-on-Sea, Kent, 1934. One of the few International Style buildings in Britain, this was commissioned by the Labour mayor of Bexhill for the benefit of the townspeople.

ing at Black Mountains College, Gropius was appointed to head the architecture department at Harvard in 1938 and arranged for Breuer to teach with him there. Mies van der Rohe headed the architecture department at the Illinois Institute of Technology (then the Armour Institute). Moholy-Nagy set up a new Bauhaus in Chicago with the intention of continuing the German experiment. The influence of these designers on American architecture after World War II was immense.

## INNOVATION AND FRANK LLOYD WRIGHT

Innovation between the wars tends to be judged on a scale of the adoption of the tenets of the International Style, and its supremacy after 1945 has tended to eclipse many of the innovations that took place during the 1930s outside the movement. The works of architects such as Frank Lloyd Wright, Buckminster Fuller and Alvar Aalto display major advances in design which have had important repercussions on present-day architecture.

The innovations of Buckminster Fuller followed technology and ignored both political and social realities. His experiments in house design took Le Corbusier's idea of a 'machine for living in' to its logical conclusion, with efficiency of production and operation his main criteria. His Dymaxion House (1927) was planned for the factory production line, as an aluminum and glass hexagonal block around a central core of services, with the ultimate in labor-saving devices, including an automatic laundry which ironed and stored the clean clothes. He argued that his results were far closer to the functional and antihistorical aims of the International Style architects than their own stylized simplicity, and compared the effects of their architecture to the tricks of a children's magician.

Other architects, who had embraced the International Style during the 1930s, developed personal styles based on more traditional ideas. Niemeyer's later buildings in Brazil show a move away from the rigid tenets of the International Style toward more idiosyncratic designs, strongly influenced by local culture. The Casino, Pampulha (1942) reflects the wealth of its clientele in its use of rich materials and the design contrasts cubic and organic forms. In the church of São Francisco, Pampulha (1939-43) he developed these ideas, combining mosaics, in bright traditional colors, with curving and rectilinear forms into a design which was decidedly modern but a far cry from the austerity of the International Style. A similar pattern was followed by Aalto in Finland. Aalto's architecture of the 1930s shows a return to the Finnish tradition of wood and other natural materials rather than the concrete of his earlier buildings. He had used wood in the ceiling of the lecture hall of the Viipuri Library and experimented further with the use of traditional materials in the modern idiom, in his own house at Munkkiniemi (1936) and the Finnish Pavilion for the Paris Exhibition (1937). Through his friendship with Harry and Mairea Gullichsøn, heiress to a timber business, he was then commissioned to design the Villa Mairea, Noormarkku (1938-9), which shows how far Aalto had progressed from the International Style. Using wood, local stone and brick he designed a house around a kidney-shaped swimming pool, employing curved and angular blocks and combining traditional Finnish design with modern abstraction in a way that rejected the rigidity of the International Style and anticipated American developments of the 1980s.

Perhaps the greatest innovations in style at this time occur in the works of Frank Lloyd Wright. After the murder of his wife and children and the destruction of Taliesin, Wright left America to take up a commission for the Imperial Hotel, Tokyo (1916-22). This was a major structural triumph for him with its floor of huge cantilevered concrete slabs, resting on mushroom piers sunk into the mud below, which acted as shock absorbers and enabled the hotel to withstand the terrible 1923 earthquake. Wright also designed a series of houses for wealthy Californian patrons, showing the influence of pre-Columbian civilizations on his work. The Barnsdall House, Hollywood (1917-22), built for the millionaire's daughter, Aline Barnsdall, was decorated with a stylized hollyhock, the patron's favorite flower. The massive simplicity of this building, reminiscent of Mayan architecture, was repeated in the Millard House. Pasadena (1923), for Mrs George M Millard. This was the first of a series of houses Wright built in the Los Angeles area using standardized concrete blocks joined with metal strands, a technique he called 'textile construction.' Like the Barnsdall House, they were decorated with stylized geometrical relief patterns of pre-Columbian inspiration. Wright aimed to design unique houses specifically for their individual sites using standardized units, quite unlike the system proposed by the International Stylists. Le Corbusier, for example, aimed for a design that would impose a standard solution regardless of variations in site or climate. Most of these houses were supervised by Wright's son, Lloyd, who had a thriving practice designing private houses in Hollywood and was influenced by the techniques and stylized decoration of his father.

In 1924 Wright separated from his third wife, marrying again the following year. The decade

**Below:** Aalto, Villa Mairea, Noormarkku, Finland, 1938-9. After a brief flirtation with the International Style, Aalto returned to the Finnish vernacular tradition, using wood and stone as building materials.

1924-34, although poor in practice, was rich in theoretical projects, especially the development of his ideas on town planning. Wright was very much in favor of industrialization, but disliked its effects on the average American city. He published his first book on town planning, *The Disappearing City*, in 1932, based on a project, Broadacre City, in which he sought to decentralize the population, breaking the dramatic differences between town and country. In creating a more even distribution of the population, he hoped to establish a more harmonious relationship between man and nature, impossible, as Wright recognized, before the mass ownership of the automobile. He foresaw the development of an egalitarian culture in the United States as a result of this decentralization, which he called 'Usonia.' This term was coined by Wright in 1928 and it had strong utopian overtones, which were incorporated into his designs for Broadacre City (first exhibited 1935). The scheme allowed for all the social amenities, accommodation, services and industries one would expect to find in a town-planning project of the period but his emphasis on decentralization yet again set him apart from Le Corbusier, whose own scheme for an ideal city was based on the principle of increasing population density toward the center.

Wright's prewar experiments with interior spatial construction influenced many architects, particularly in California, with its tradition of innovation in architecture which is often underrated. Irving Gill, who had trained with Sullivan in Chicago, was much influenced by the Hispanic traditions of architecture in California. His Walter Luther Dodge House (1916; demolished), built of reinforced concrete, was an asymmetrical combination of cubic forms, which expressed the interior arrangement of rooms. Clearly inspired by Mediterranean prototypes, it lacked the orthodoxy of the modern movement. Rudolph Schindler, who had emigrated from Austria in 1914, worked with Wright in Chicago and moved to Los Angeles. One of Schindler's earliest projects in California was the Schindler Studio House, Hollywood (1921-2), built as a double house for himself and Clyde Chase, an engineer. The two families had separate accommodation with a communal garage and vegetable garden. Wright's influence shows in the spatial planning of rooms and gardens. Schindler designed a sunken garden and lawns for each family, deliberately diffusing the relationship between interior and exterior. The structure of concrete slabs with glass between shows Schindler's interest in modern materials but it is lighter than Wright's style. His Beach

**Below:** Wright, Barnsdall House, Los Angeles, California, 1917-22. Also called Hollyhock House, this building shows Wright's imaginative use of his patron's favorite flower.

**Left:** Wright, Charles Ennis House, Los Angeles, California, 1924. Unlike the modern movement in Europe, Wright's innovative buildings were inspired by past styles, in this case pre-Columbian architecture in Mexico.

**Right:** Schindler, Lovell Beach House, Los Angeles, California, 1925-6. Schindler's personal style, which owed much to the influence of Wright, did not conform with the strict theories of the modern movement.

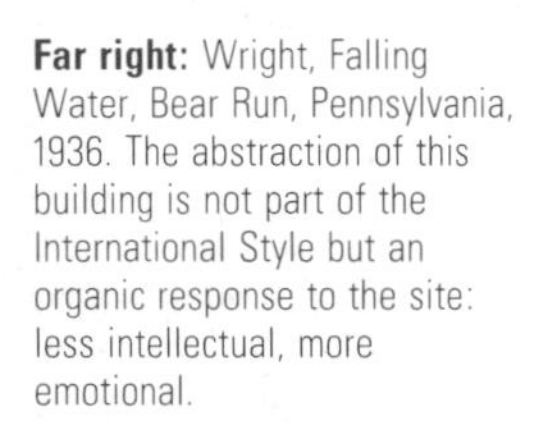

**Far right:** Wright, Falling Water, Bear Run, Pennsylvania, 1936. The abstraction of this building is not part of the International Style but an organic response to the site: less intellectual, more emotional.

**Below:** Wright, Johnson Wax Co, Administration Building, Racine, Wisconsin, 1936-9. The interior was lit through the gaps between the circular capitals, enhancing the fantasy of a forest of columns.

House for Dr Lovell, Newport Beach (1925-6), experiments more fully with Wright's spatial ideas. The basic structure consists of five concrete frames with the main body of the house raised above the beach and the vertical concrete supports are balanced with strong horizontal emphasis of the balconies. His Buck House, Los Angeles (1934) and Fitzpatrick House, Hollywood (1936) further explore the subtle interrelationship between exterior and interior. Like Wright, Schindler was a critic of the International Style. He disliked the standardized forms of modern architecture, criticizing them for imposing the same rigidity on architects as the traditions they sought to replace. Other architects who had come under the influence of Wright felt the same way. Bruce Goff began his career in the 1930s with a series of houses in the Chicago area. His Colmorgan House, Glenview (1937), with its heavy overhanging roofline balanced by a large central core, shows the clear influence of Wright, although the interior is very conventional.

Wright's attitude to the International Style was ambivalent. His beliefs in the importance of the machine as the tool of the modern architect had been of prime importance to the early figures of the modern movement. However, he felt that the machine had taken over as the master of man, the standardization of the houses of the International Style imitating the machine rather than using it. In a series of lectures at Princeton (1930) he criticized these houses under the title of 'The Cardboard House.' Starting with an anthropomorphic view of the house, likening electric wiring to the nervous system and plumbing to the digestive system, he criticized modern architecture on the grounds that it did not take the organic nature of architecture into consideration, but sought to impose universal solutions. He rather frivolously suggested that they should trim all the trees to match! Wright's

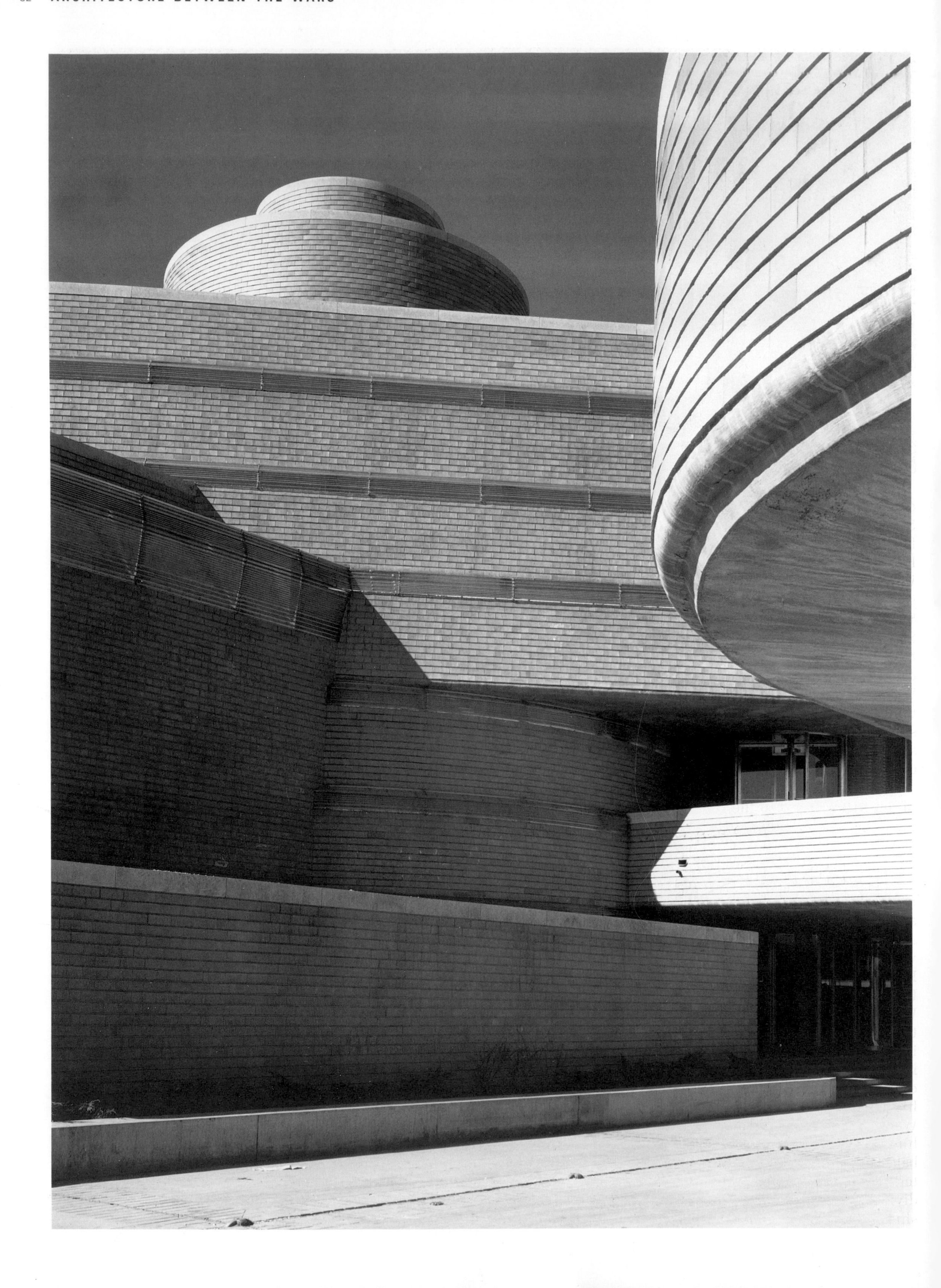

**Above:** Wright, Taliesin West, Scottsville, Arizona, 1938. Unobtrusive and asymmetric, Wright designed his house, workshop and offices to blend in with the desert landscape.

criticism of the uniformity of the International Style can be seen in his Usonian houses of the late 1930s, starting with the Herbert Jacobs House, Westmorland, Wisconsin (1937). Wright showed how cheapness did not necessarily result in standardization. The house cost $5500 to design and build in contrast to $35,000 for the Robie House in 1909. It was built on a concrete slab with walls of prefabricated plywood panels inset with glass doors. Wright had hoped to build many groups of these houses, but only one group was commissioned, for teachers at Michigan State University. The only completed house was for Alma Goetsch and K Winkler, Okemos (1939).

Wright's emotional and financial problems of the 1920s abated in the 1930s with another marriage and the setting up of an educational camp at Taliesin West, which was part farm and part architectural school. This stability gave him the base from which to reemerge dramatically on to the *avant-garde* architectural stage, with two buildings which, by any standard, rank as masterpieces. Aged 68, he was commissioned by a Pittsburgh millionaire, Edgar J Kaufmann, to design his house at Bear Run, Pennsylvania (1936) and by the Johnson Wax Corporation to design their Administration Building, Racine, Wisconsin (1936-9). It is indicative of Wright's genius that he could start his career again at such an age and with a level of creativity that at least paralleled the works of his youth. The Kaufmann House, Falling Water, is literally poised above a waterfall with huge cantilevered concrete slabs held in balance by the central chimney core. The interior and exterior merge through glass walls divided with thin metal strips and the relationship between the house and its setting is expressed in the aggressive projection of the slabs, designed to reflect the boulders in the pools below. The importance of a relationship between the house and its site was stressed by Wright as a crucial element in his 'organic' approach to architecture. Both these buildings display Wright's exploitation of the structural potential of concrete. The Johnson Wax Administration Building is supported by a forest of concrete mushroom columns, tapering at their bases into bronze 'shoes.' A far cry from the skeleton structure of the International Style, but the effect of freeing the walls from their traditional load-bearing role is precisely the same. As if in conscious criticism of the cubic simplicity of the International Style, Wright based the design of the Johnson Wax Administration Building on the circle, from the rounded corners of the building itself to the furniture, designed specifically by Wright.

Wright experimented with a variety of shapes in his later buildings. He used the circle again in the Ralph Jester House, Palos Verdes, California (1938), and his project for St Mark's Tower apartment block, New York (1929), is based on elongated hexagons composed into a cross, producing a dynamic design quite unlike the serenity and balance of his earlier houses (it was finally built in 1956 as the Price Tower, Bartlesville, Oklahoma). In his own house, Taliesin West, Scottsville, Arizona (1938), he combined angles of 45 degrees and 90 degrees in the plan and this is echoed in the curiously angled roofline. In deliberately rejecting the authoritarianism of the International Style, Wright set himself apart from the mainstream of architectural design after World War II but, like Niemeyer and Aalto, his approach to architecture set an important precedent.

**Left:** Wright, Johnson Wax Co, Administration Building, Racine, Wisconsin, 1936-9. Wright's preference for round forms shows his dislike of the uniform angularity of the International Style.

# 3/THE SUCCESS OF THE INTERNATIONAL STYLE

Mies van der Rohe, Seagram Building, New York City, 1954-8.

World War II destroyed Europe's traditional position as the center of world power. Physically devastated, economically prostrate and politically divided, Europe's control of world affairs slackened. Immediately after the war, Germany had been divided temporarily into four sectors, under the control of the major allies, Britain, France, the United States and Russia. The political face of Europe was radically altered with the permanent domination of Russia in the eastern sector. The breakup of the old empires of Britain, France, Belgium and the Netherlands further diminished Europe's prewar control of world affairs. The process had begun before 1945, but under American pressure the dissolution speeded up. India and Pakistan gained independence from Britain in 1947 and her African colonies soon followed, although British interest was retained by the establishment of the Commonwealth under the nominal leadership of the King. Indonesia became independent from the Netherlands in 1947 and France gave up Vietnam, Cambodia and Laos in 1949. The redefining of political boundaries led to chaos in many of the old colonies. The partition of India and Pakistan in 1947 resulted in a terrible bloodbath as Hindus fought Muslims (India's birth pains when she was destined to become the largest democracy in the world). In 1950-2 Russia fought the American-dominated troops of the United Nations for control of Korea. Britain's reluctance to relinquish her status as a world power resulted in an invasion of Egypt in 1956 to stop Nasser's nationalization of the Suez canal. The determination of the Zionists to create an independent Jewish state in Palestine led to bitter fighting between Arab and Jew. A series of economic or political alliances on a regional basis replaced the old empires, notably the Council of Europe (1949), NATO (1949) and ultimately the European Economic Community set up through the Treaty of Rome (1958). These alliances were essentially co-operative, not the unequal unions of Empire.

The United States emerged from the war as a leading world power. The old League of Nations had failed and it was superseded by the United Nations, whose charter was signed in 1945. New York City replaced Geneva as the new guarantee of peace. American economic power had been strengthened by the war, and her economic assistance to Europe after the war – in the form of the Marshall Plan (1947) – emphasized her new and dominant role. Russia's postwar political position was considerably strengthened by her new areas of control and, together, the United States and the Soviet Union shared the vacuum left by Europe's inability to dominate world affairs. The prewar American policy of isolation from European affairs irrevocably changed in response to Soviet domination of Eastern Europe. The Cold War that resulted, led to the McCarthy witchhunt for left-wing sympathizers (1952-4) and ultimately to the erection of the Berlin Wall (1961) and the Cuba crisis (1962).

During the war, European allies and the United States had cooperated as equal partners. After the war, the differences in their positions were marked. Europe had neither the economic nor the political power to maintain her prewar position of world power. Class distinctions had been blurred by the war and this contributed to the Labour landslide victory in the British election of 1945. Nationalization of Europe's major industries and the persistence of wartime austerity (food rationing was not lifted in Britain until 1954) contrasted with the consumer boom experienced in the United States. By 1963 91 percent of American households owned a washing machine, only 40 percent did so in Britain. The devastation of the war made reconstruction the key architectural issue in Europe, and the scale of the problem led to the novel development of extensive state patronage, necessity dictating style. By contrast, architecture in the United States was dominated almost exclusively by private patronage. Commercial wealth and political power were expressed in expensive images, and America's domination of the architectural scene reflected her position in the world.

### THE BAUHAUS ÉMIGRÉS

Hitler's anti-Semitic and antisocialist policies changed the face of American culture. No longer a backwater, America was suddenly the center of the modern artistic world with composers like Schönberg, artists like Ernst, Mondrian and Chagall, together with most of the key figures from the Bauhaus: Gropius, Breuer, Mies van der Rohe, Moholy-Nagy and Albers. The International Style had been rejected before the war because of its socialist, if not communist associations, its lack of reverence for tradition and its insistence on an industrial aesthetic, but Hitler's policies brought about a complete change of attitude. Anything Hitler thought was bad, automatically must be good for everyone else and the International Style suddenly represented freedom from oppression and the style of the new age.

The Bauhaus architects were quickly appointed to important positions within the academic institutions of America. Mies van der Rohe became Dean of Architecture at the newly formed Illinois Institute of Technology (IIT), Moholy-Nagy set up a new Bauhaus in Chicago and Albers was appointed to the Fine Arts Department at Yale. Gropius' post as Chairman of the Department of Architecture at the Harvard Graduate School, and Breuer's subsequent appointment there, had come about largely as a result of the influence of Joseph

**Above:** Gropius, Gropius House, Lincoln, Massachusetts, 1938. The first modern house in the area. Gropius' appointment as Chairman of the Architecture Department at Harvard ensured the success of the International Style.

Hudnut, Dean of Harvard School of Design. These appointments revolutionized architectural education in America.

Relying heavily on classical tradition, outlined by the Roman architectural theorist Vitruvius, architects since the Renaissance had been educated in the principles of design, proportion and decorum by the study of the monuments of the past, with a strong emphasis on draftsmanship. This resulted in only a superficial knowledge of construction, deemed the province of the engineer. Initially an apprentice system, formal architectural education, developed in schools and universities, but the emphasis on draftsmanship and the study of historical styles was the same. The arrival of the Bauhaus teachers changed all this.

Gropius and the others introduced the new conceptual and intellectual approach to design which had been developed at the Bauhaus, relegating draftsmanship and the study of the architecture of the past to the bin of irrelevance. Cultural education was replaced by an emphasis on social responsibilities and technology, blurring the traditional distinctions between the architect and social scientist or engineer. The architect's task was to interpret the social needs of inhabitants into designs, and Gropius stressed the importance of standardization and group collaboration rather than individual achievement.

Gropius continued his prewar research into the problems of low-cost housing in partnership with Konrad Wachsmann, a pioneer in construction technology. They worked on prefabrication, in particular the 'packaged-house system' for the General Panel Corporation. In 1946 Gropius put his principles to the test by going into partnership with a group of young architects to form The Architects' Collaborative (TAC) and their first major commission was a new Graduate Center at Harvard (1949-50). The layout of the residential blocks was based on the traditional Oxbridge pattern of courtyards, but the buildings had an unmistakable Bauhaus flavor, with their flat roofs, reinforced-concrete and steel construction, and strip windows. The use of *pilotis* shows the influence of Le Corbusier and the only traditional American feature was the employment of light-colored bricks as infill.

The Harvard Graduate Center signified a radical change. University building throughout the interwar years had been remarkable for its conservatism, closely following the traditional models of Oxford and Cambridge. The challenge of new ideas was expressed in a new form and this was not restricted to intellectual circles. Commercial architecture was also responding to the new ideas, showing how quickly the International Style had been accepted as an appropriate image for postwar

**Right:** Gropius & TAC, Harvard University Graduate Center, Cambridge, Mass, 1949-50. Prewar university architecture in America had been remarkable for its adherence to tradition. The arrival of Gropius and other architects decisively changed this.

America. Gropius designed relatively few commercial buildings. His Pan Am Building, New York (1958), illustrates the problem of adapting the social relevance of the International Style to the image required for commercial patrons and Gropius' lack of success at doing that. His considerable influence on the spread of the style lay in his presence, his theories and his teaching.

Mies van der Rohe was far more successful in adapting his style to express the image of the consumer society, and his impact on the next

**Below:** Gropius & TAC, Pan Am Building, New York City, 1958. An early attempt to adapt the International Style, with all its socialist connotations, for images of capitalist America.

**Left:** Mies van der Rohe, Crown Hall, IIT, Chicago, Illinois, 1952-6. Fire regulations made a sham of structural honesty. The actual structure is encased in concrete and we see a fake structure welded on top.

**Below:** Mies van der Rohe, Lake Shore Drive apartments, Chicago, Illinois, 1949-51. The International Style made no distinction between building types. Here there are no visual clues to tell whether this is a block of apartments or offices.

generation of architects was enormous. The extreme simplicity and elegance of his earlier works had a glamor, lacking in the works of Le Corbusier and Gropius, which developed easily into the austere impersonal imagery we associate with his style. It has been copied and interpreted all over the Western world, a measure of his success as the architect of capitalism. One of his earliest commissions in the United States was for the new Illinois Institute of Technology, Ann Arbor, Michigan (1939, 1942-56), brought about by the merging of the Armour and the Lewis Institutes. The plan is asymmetrical with a series of buildings, some on *pilotis*, arranged along a central axis. The rectangular blocks, faced with glass curtain walls held in their black-painted metal frames, look like functional factory buildings and display the visual purity of his style. But this is all show. Fire regulations demanded that the structural members must be enclosed in concrete and the visible 'structure' turns out to be a mask welded on top. This determination to show the structure of the building makes a mockery of the Bauhaus tenet of structural honesty, but the whole complex has an elegance which undoubtedly appealed.

Mies' Apartment Blocks on Lake Shore Drive, Chicago, Illinois (1949-51), have the same uncompromising forms in both plan and elevation, the two being rectangular blocks placed at right angles. Again the steel skeleton structure is hidden in concrete casing and

**Above:** Mies van der Rohe, Farnsworth House, Fox River, Illinois, 1949-51. A Glass Box, which was the ultimate in minimal purity.

**Right:** Mies van der Rohe, Seagram Building, New York City, 1954-8. The epitome of the commercial image – a geometric box, austere and impersonal, copied in every business center in the world.

expressed on the exterior by I-beams welded on to the façades. His overriding concern for form shows in a lack of practical consideration of the function of the building and the needs of its inhabitants. The apartments vary considerably in desirability, depending on which direction they face, but his original intention for open-plan apartments was too much for the inhabitants, who vetoed the idea, and they were divided traditionally, into rooms. One of the few buildings where he was honest about its structure was the Farnsworth House, Fox River, Illinois (1949-51), a weekend home for Dr Edith Farnsworth. It is startling in its simplicity. The building consists of two slabs, roof and floor, hovering above ground and supported by I-beams. A small intermediary slab makes the step from floor to ground. The house appears to float in space and the sense of unreality is emphasized by walls of glass. The interior is designed around a closed central core containing the bathrooms, fireplace and other services. The idea of luxury in simplicity, or in Miesian terms 'less is more,' had appeared in his earlier buildings like the Tugendhat House, but in the United States it soon became a cult.

Cold impersonality and supremacy of form may pose problems for private housing, but it was exactly the image that the big corporations wanted. Mies' Seagram Building, New York (1954-8), designed in collaboration with Philip Johnson, is sited opposite McKim, Mead and White's Racquet Club on Park Avenue, symbols of the old America and the new. The formal classicism of the Racquet Club contrasts with the abstract classical simplicity of the Seagram Building, with its sheer glass and metal walls welded to the structure beneath. The wealth of the corporation is expressed in bronze-colored columns and dark amber glass, its impersonal and all-powerful image conveyed in uniformity and monumentality.

The imposition of form as order on chaos was crucial to Mies. His use of structural forms as 'decoration' is similar to the Roman decorative use of the Greek structural system of columns and entablature, with the same intention of conveying the message of the original style without conforming to its tenets. Mies' architecture has further classical analogies in the rigid order, regularity and simplicity he imposed on his façades and their post and lintel construction.

AL SCHACHT'S

**Left:** Skidmore, Owings & Merrill (SOM), Lever House, New York City, 1950-2. One of the earliest skyscrapers of the consumer boom in postwar America, this building adapted the rectangular block of the UN Secretariat, rising without setbacks and decisively abandoning prewar practice.

**Right:** SOM, Chase Manhattan Bank, New York City, 1957-61. Toward the end of the 1950s, skyscrapers became higher as a direct result of rising costs and taxes. Twenty-one stories of Lever House were dwarfed by the 60 stories of the Chase Manhattan Bank.

The importance of Gropius, Mies van der Rohe and the other Bauhaus émigrés to the development of postwar architecture cannot be underestimated. Gropius' theoretical contribution and Mies' adaptation of the International Style in practice were crucial, and the purist impersonal image was taken up wholesale.

### IMAGE, TECHNOLOGY and COMMERCE

The first postwar skyscraper in New York was for the UN Headquarters. It is fitting that the new role of the International Style as the image of freedom from oppression was first expressed in this symbol of future peace, rather than in a commercial commission. The United Nations Charter was signed in 1945, and in 1947 the UN appointed a committee to advise on the design of its headquarters which, true to its international character, included such eminent non-Americans as Le Corbusier and Niemeyer. Le Corbusier's plan was for two skyscrapers, vertical slabs, set at 90 degrees, with a horizontal slab beside them as a visual balance. The three buildings were to rest on *pilotis* and separately house the Secretariat, the General Assembly and the Meeting Halls. The final plan, by Harrison and Abramowitz (1948) reversed the arrangement, with one vertical slab for the Secretariat and the other bodies in two horizontal blocks. The Secretariat building is glazed only on the two broad façades, their uniformity relieved by three thicker bands of windows, based on Le Corbusier's original articulation of his own façades.

World War II helped to revive America from the Depression of the 1930s, and corporate profits doubled between 1940 and 1945, encouraging a rise in the standard of living. As the country had suffered little war damage, postwar readjustment was rapid and hastened by the enormous demand for consumer goods. The ensuing economic boom gave rise to the term *The Affluent Society,* coined by the economist J K Galbraith in 1958. In architectural terms it gave rise to an equivalent boom in commercial building, universally adopting the style of the new and free America. In theory, technological advances could have allowed a far greater freedom of expression for the architects of the 1950s, particularly in comparison with the pioneers of skyscraper design of the 1890s. However, this freedom was restricted by the importance of conformity to the now-established taste for the impersonal image and also by economic viability. The International Style had developed out of an attempt to provide well-designed but low-cost housing, making a virtue out of the necessity for standardization. This 'virtue' was exploited in the development of a style that had none of the prewar socialist idealism but was motivated by the purely commercial need to provide maximum space at minimum cost to gain maximum profit. The resulting buildings, with their industrial references to efficiency and organization, and lack of historical detail, were potent symbols for the new commercial age.

Apart from standardization, other features derived from the prewar International Style

**Far left:** Harrison & Abramowitz, UN Secretariat, New York City, 1948. Hitler's dislike of the International Style gave it the respectability it had lacked in prewar Europe. The image of freedom from oppression, it was ideal for the new symbol of peace.

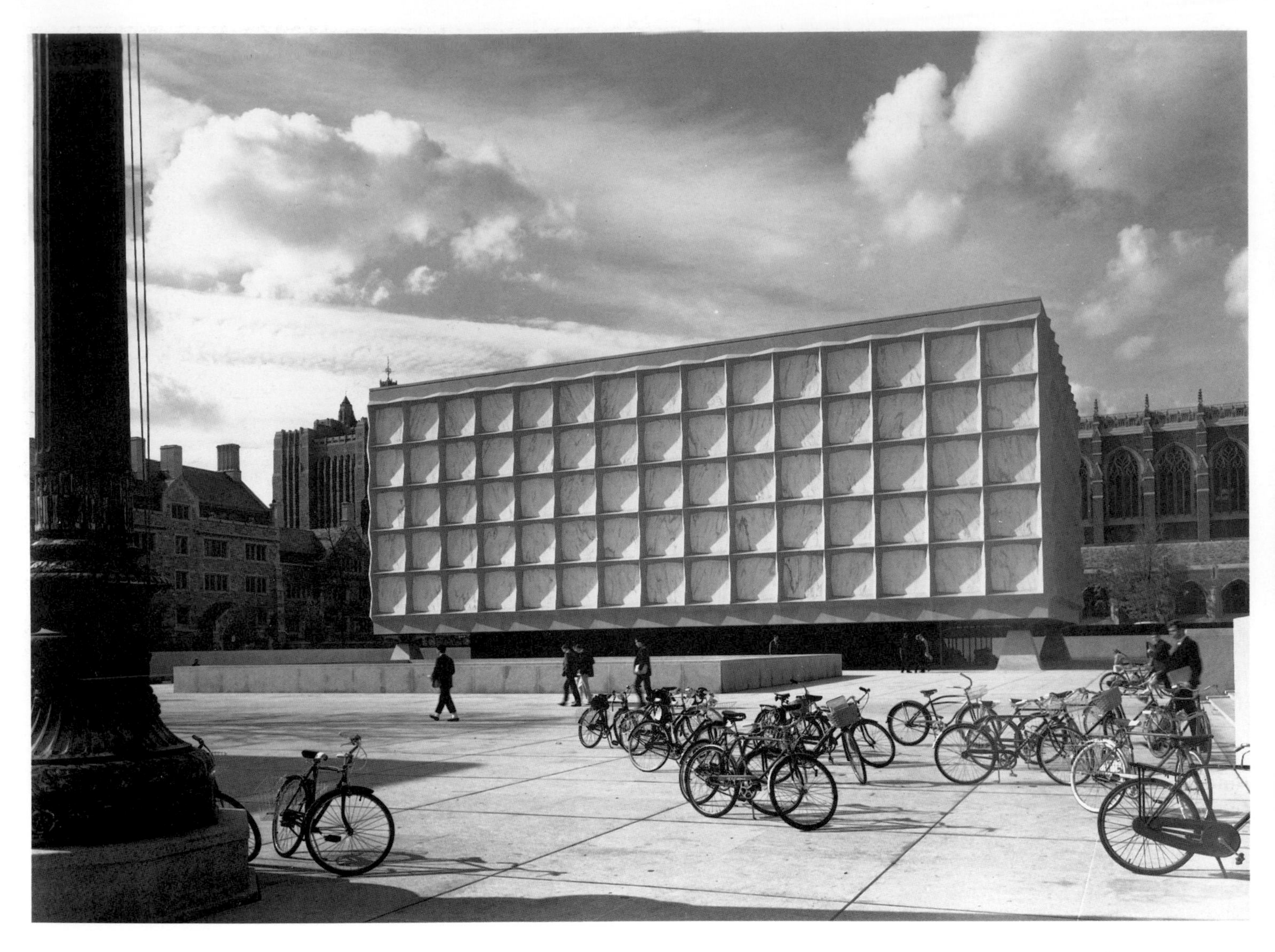

**Above:** SOM, Beinecke Library, Yale University, New Haven, Connecticut, 1964. This façade was designed specifically to allow for the regulation of the interior atmosphere.

included skeleton structures and *pilotis*. One of its major characteristics has been the development of the curtain wall, which had been used before the war but was exploited extensively afterward. Mies' curtain wall for the Seagram Building followed the examples of Pietro Belluschi's Equitable Savings and Loan Association Building, Portland, Oregon (1944-8) and Lever House, New York (1950-2), by Skidmore, Owings and Merrill (SOM). Lever House, following the design of the isolated UN Secretariat, rises without setbacks on a small part of its site, setting the style for later skyscrapers and in direct contrast to prewar practice. The remainder of the site at Lever House is covered by an enclosed 'plaza,' its walls supported on *pilotis*. Later skyscrapers, such as the Seagram Building, were fronted by open, more public spaces.

The firm of Skidmore, Owings and Merrill marks a major development in the history of the architect. Hitchcock has noted that American architects began working anonymously under the umbrella of an architectural firm, a practice encouraged by Gropius. It is significant that these firms were commercial organizations, operating in exactly the same way as their patrons. To distinguish themselves further from tradition, the patron was renamed 'client,' endorsing the corporate status of the architect and implying a subservient role on the part of the client. The firm of Skidmore, Owings and Merrill was founded in 1936 in Chicago and offices were opened in New York, San Francisco and Portland, Oregon. In conscious imitation of the groups of anonymous master-builders, who designed and constructed the cathedrals of the Middle Ages, it offered a wide variety of services, such as interior design, engineers, and other specialists in various fields, in addition to traditional architectural design and construction. The vast output of SOM has made the company synonymous with corporate architecture, effectively creating the standard solution to the problem of building for corporations, which has since been imitated with varying degrees of success worldwide.

The developments made by Albert Kahn in factory design between the wars were continued by architects such as Eero Saarinen in his design for the General Motors Technical Center, Warren, Michigan (1949-55). It is an enormous complex, comparable in size to Mies' IIT campus, which it also resembles stylistically. The 25 buildings are organized

around a man-made lake, and vary in size, form and articulation, but they are all constructed of glass and steel or aluminum. The façades of the blocks, with their black metal and green glass are enlivened by the brightly colored glazed brickwork, distinguishing them from the purer style of Mies van der Rohe. Two of the buildings, the Auditorium and the Water Tower use curved forms, suggesting an independence from the purism of the International Style which was developed in his later buildings. Saarinen's concern for form went a long way beyond the utilitarian industrial buildings of Albert Kahn.

**Above:** Saarinen, General Motors building, Warren, Michigan, 1949-55. A recognizable image: industrial style for an industrial complex.

**Left:** Urbahn, Roberts, Schaefer & Co, Vehicle Assembly Building, NASA, Cape Kennedy, Florida, 1958-60: modern monumentality for the image of man's conquest of space.

**Right:** Harrison, Abramowitz & Johnson, Lincoln Center, New York City, 1957-66. Modern industrial style proved inappropriate for culture and is here given an aura of plausibility with the addition of classical details.

**Far right:** Goldberg & Assocs, Marina City Flats, Chicago, Illinois, 1964-7. This complex was an attempt to revive the city center. The first 18 floors house car parks, and the apartments are above.

The International Style, developed to express a deliberate and total break with the past, was appropriate for the commercial, political and even educational images of the new order, but less successful for culture, with its roots so firmly in the past. The Lincoln Center, New York (1957-66), which was developed as part of an urban renewal program for the West Side, included the Metropolitan Opera House by Harrison, the Philharmonic Hall by Abramowitz, and the New York State Theater by Johnson. This complex of three large buildings arranged around a piazza, with its superficial references to Michelangelo's Capitol Hill in Rome in the pattern on the square and the austere arches of the Opera House, illustrates the problem of achieving monumentality with the language of the International Style.

**Below:** Johnson, Glass House, New Canaan, Connecticut, 1949-50. Based on Mies van der Rohe's Farnsworth House, this develops the modern concept of luxury in simplicity.

Philip Johnson, who collaborated with Hitchcock on the catalogue for the International Style exhibition, studied architecture at Harvard under Gropius and Breuer, graduating in 1943. He worked with Mies van der Rohe on the Seagram Building and was profoundly influenced by Mies' success in adapting the International Style to modern commercial demands. His own house, the Glass House, New Canaan, Connecticut (1949-50), was clearly derived from Mies' Farnsworth House, a transparent box with its metal frame enclosing a space broken only by a central service element. He developed this geometrically purist style in the Rockefeller Guest House, New York (1950), and the Boissonas House, New Canaan (1955-6). His later commissions, for example the Williams-Proctor Institute, Utica, New York (1957-60), and the Kline Laboratory, Yale University (1962-6), have less of the geometrical purity but show how his impersonal, clinical style evolved into a pursuit of visual perfection, disguising the structure of his buildings.

This minimalist approach to house design was taken up by some Californian architects. Neutra's Kaufmann House, Palm Springs, California (1945-7), designed for the same patron as Wright's Falling Water, is a series of glass boxes, the simple rectangular plan of Mies and Johnson replaced by a more complicated arrangement of three unequal wings containing bedrooms and services laid out around a central living space. The Eames House, Santa Monica, California (1947-9), by Charles and

**Above:** Johnson, Boissonas House, New Canaan, Connecticut, 1955-6. Further experiments with form led Johnson to develop some bizarre solutions.

**Below:** Neutra, Kaufmann Desert House, Palm Springs, California, 1945-7. Another glass box, but the interior atmosphere needs careful controlling to cope with the intense desert heat.

Ray Eames, was one of a series of Case Study Houses sponsored by a local journal, *California Arts and Architecture*, with the aim of developing the new materials and techniques. These steel-and-glass structures, by architects like C Ellwood, P Koenig and R Soriano, were influenced by Miesian concepts of simplicity and standardization in reaction to the eclectic vernacular styles current in California.

## LE CORBUSIER

Le Corbusier was the only one of the major prewar architects left in Europe by 1939. His experience of the war was more direct than the Bauhaus architects in America and his enthusiasm for the machine was considerably weakened. After 1945 he had to adapt to the demands of a society torn by war, very different from the consumer boom of America. Whereas Mies van der Rohe desired to impose rational and methodical order on chaos, Le Corbusier preferred to express that chaos in his postwar designs, experimenting with new means of expression in an attempt to create forms that relied less heavily on the cult of the machine. The geometrical purity of his earlier works was replaced by a more sculptural approach to design. He developed the use of unfinished concrete, *béton brut*, taken directly from the molds. This was very influential, especially in Britain and the development of Brutalist architecture. His recognition of the rough texture and innate sculptural potential of concrete shows an Arts and Crafts concern for truth to materials. Another feature of his later work was the 'sun break,' *brise-soleil*, which increased the textural quality of his façades, showing how far he had developed from the simplicity and purity of the Citrohan houses.

During the 1930s Le Corbusier had worked on the theoretical replanning of existing city centers such as Paris, Algiers, Buenos Aires and São Paolo, developing the concept of *Une Ville Contemporaine* at a more practical level. His earliest postwar commissions involved

**Left:** Charles & Ray Eames, The Eames House, Santa Monica, California, 1947-9. Inspired by Japanese architecture, this house was constructed with interchangeable prefabricated units.

urban reconstruction and the provision of low-cost housing schemes, which embodied many of these ideas. He was commissioned to replan La Rochelle-Pallice and Saint-Dié (never realized) and to design a housing project in Marseilles.

In the design of the Unité d'Habitation at Marseilles (1946-52), Le Corbusier was given a free hand by the government to implement his radical ideas on housing, based on the socialist ideals of the International Style in a way that Gropius and Mies van der Rohe were less able

**Left:** Le Corbusier, Unité d'Habitation, Marseilles, France, 1946-52. The demand for low-cost housing in postwar Europe gave Le Corbusier the chance to put his socialist ideals into practice, an opportunity denied to the Bauhaus émigrés in America.

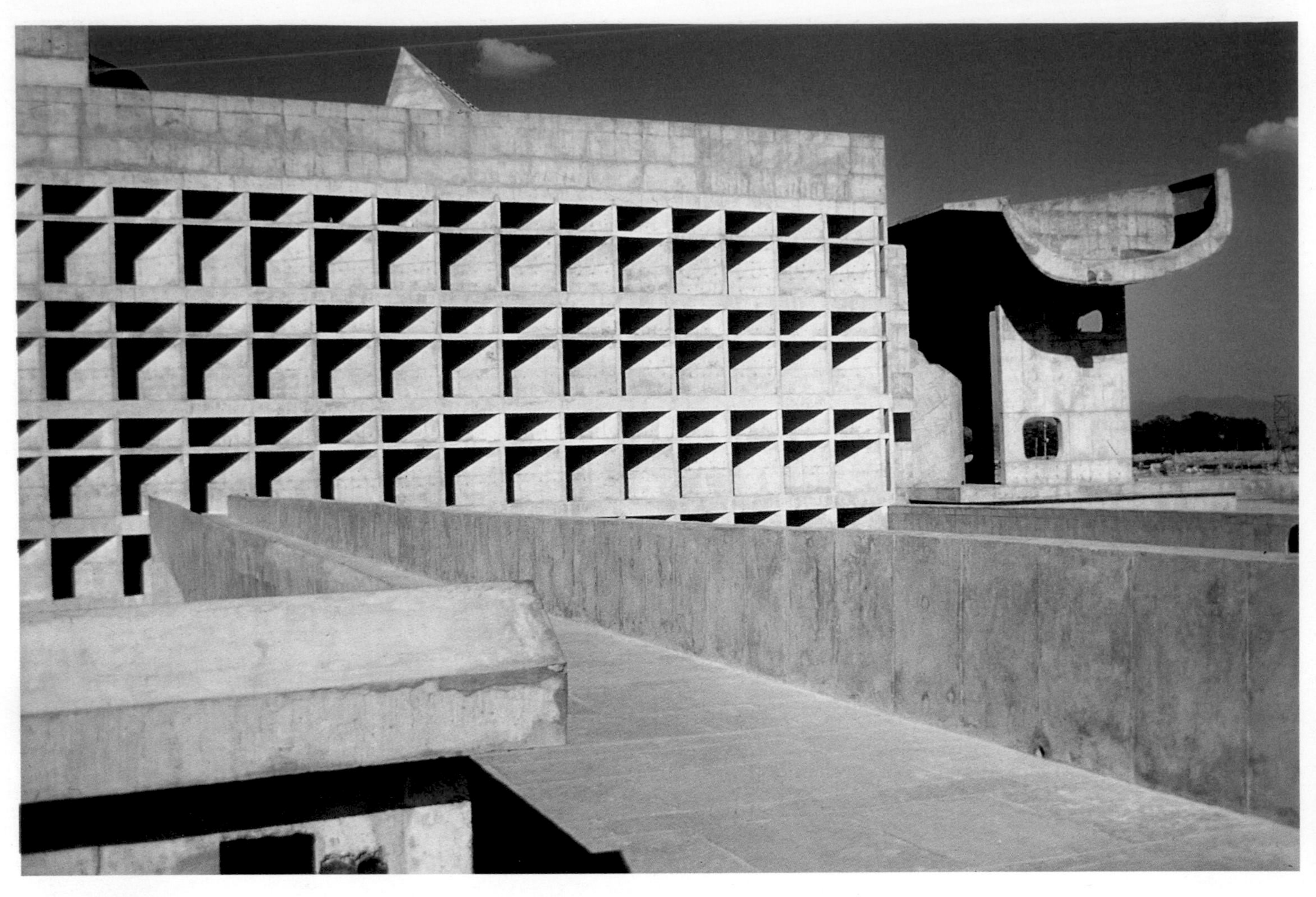

**Above:** Le Corbusier and Fry & Drew, Legislative Assembly, Chandigarh, India, 1959-62. Rough concrete and heavy, curved forms show how Le Corbusier had moved away from the geometrical purity of his prewar architecture.

to do. The block contains many of the stylistic characteristics of his prewar architecture, such as *pilotis* and double-story living-rooms, but the purist forms of his earlier villas were replaced by the more sculptural effects of rough concrete and *brise-soleil*. The block contained 337 apartments ranging from studio rooms to units for families with children, and an interior 'street,' identified from the outside by a different window pattern in the middle of the block. Apart from shopping arcades, the block contained many other amenities including a crêche, kindergarten, gymnasium, restaurant and a swimming-pool on the roof, attempting to create a self-contained community. These 'vertical garden cities,' as Le Corbusier described the blocks, aimed deliberately at maximum privacy for each family, balanced with a community spirit engendered by the provision of services. Le Corbusier was not given the opportunity to design many of these housing units, but the few examples were extremely influential. The Marseilles block was improved on at Nantes-Reze (1952-5) with its shops on the ground floor, instead of in the 'streets,' increasing outside access. Other Unités were erected at Briey-en-Forêt (1957), Firminy (1967) and for the Interbau Exhibition at Charlottenburg, Berlin (1956).

Le Corbusier was commissioned to design the administrative capital of the Punjab at Chandigarh (the former capital, Lahore, was ceded to Pakistan when it split from India in 1947). The administrative center was to contain three main buildings: the Courts of Justice (1952-6), the Secretariat (1952-8) and the Legislative Assembly (1959-62). He was nominally in charge of the whole city but the rest of the work, notably the planning, was undertaken by two English architects, Jane Drew and E Maxwell Fry, together with Le Corbusier's cousin and partner, Pierre Jeanneret. The design of the Courts of Justice shows how clearly Le Corbusier was concerned with the practical problems of site and climate. The main façade of the building, fronting on to a stretch of water, is covered with concrete *brise-soleil*, as he had used in his Unité d'Habitation, and the heavy rounded roof jutting out over the façade acts as an umbrella/parasol, sheltering the building from both the heavy monsoon rain and the strong sun. Le Corbusier was undoubtedly influenced by the spirit of classical architecture, but the Chandigarh complex achieves the monumentality appropriate to its function without calling upon classical prototypes for its stylistic inspiration.

Le Corbusier's best-known and most controversial postwar building was the church of Notre-Dame-du-Haut, Ronchamp (1950-4). It has been criticized for its irrationality by the supporters of Le Corbusier's prewar 'rational-

**Above:** Le Corbusier, Notre-Dame-du-Haut, Ronchamp, France, 1950-4: difficult to recognize as a church but a symbol of modern architectural style.

ism' and praised for its successful organization of space by converts to the new style. Either way it is a landmark in architectural history. His use of curves shows a complete change from his earlier geometric style and suggests a primitive, mystical inspiration. Equally carefully composed, the obvious logic of the earlier buildings is replaced here by an arranged informality, far more expressive, if not Expressionist. He created a church which aimed to convey the dual qualities of Christianity through its form, by contrasting the peaceful and spiritual interior with the bold and aggressive exterior. The small apertures of the exterior windows open up through the thickness of the wall, reminiscent of the arrow slits in Crusader castles, and create mystical tunnels of light inside, in the best tradition of the Gothic cathedral. Visually, however, the building is the antithesis of Gothic design, a rough and heavy exterior with contrasting angular and curved forms, housing a simple cave which appears to lack structural logic. The ambiguities are deliberate and the building makes a more primitive and emotional statement about religion than the highly ordered and stylized Gothic.

The proportions of the building are governed by Le Corbusier's Modulor system, published as *Le Modulor* (1951), based on the geometric principle of the Golden Section, which had been invested with mystical powers by medieval philosophers. In his attempt to discover a proportion for standardized units that was 'a harmonious measure to the human scale,' Le Corbusier related the Golden Section to the

**Left:** Le Corbusier, Monastery of La Tourette, Eveux, near Lyons, France, 1952-60. Le Corbusier's use of *brise-soleil* and unfinished concrete gives weight and texture to the building, which lacks the uniform lightness of his prewar style.

**Above:** Le Corbusier, Carpenter Center, Harvard University, Cambridge, Mass, 1960. Le Corbusier's later buildings rejected many of the tenets of the International Style and were less popular in America.

proportions of the human body, combining both the spiritual and the physical aspects of humanity. By basing his architectural unit on the male figure, Le Corbusier was following the classical tradition from Vitruvius onward, a far cry from the industrial ethic of the International Style.

The style of his other religious commission is quite different, suggesting a recognition of the restrictiveness inherent in the uniformity of the International Style. The Dominican monastery of La Tourette, Eveux, near Lyons (1952-60; now Centre Thomas More) was built for the use of a well-ordered community. Le Corbusier respected tradition and function by grouping the cells, library, chapel and other rooms around an open cloister. He took advantage of the sloping site by placing the entrance at the higher ground level and the refectory at the lower level with a view down the hill. Like Notre-Dame-du-Haut, the whole complex is organized on his Modulor system which dictates the rhythm of the concrete struts, with the cell balconies projecting in two bands above.

Le Corbusier's exploitation of the sculptural potential of concrete showed in his hyperbolic paraboloids of precast concrete for the Philips Pavilion, Brussels World Fair (1957-8), and the composition of curved and pointed forms was intentionally designed to be acoustically and visually exciting. Le Corbusier's postwar projects show the development of some of the theoretical ideas of the prewar era, but his interpretation of those ideas had changed radically. The concept of the standard solution and uniform style had been replaced by variety and texture, which created harsher, expressive and more monumental forms in complete contrast to the technological minimalism of Mies van der Rohe and the architecture of *The Affluent Society*. Le Corbusier's influence was enormous. His writings, which were prolific, have been published worldwide and have inspired many architects and planners. His deep-seated commitment to the original ideals of the International Style, which he retained throughout his life, gave him the reputation of a rebel. His inability to compromise his beliefs has meant that his architecture has never degenerated into a mere formalism, as was the case with many of his contemporaries. His architecture, in both theory and practice, has inspired many, in particular the postwar architects in Britain.

## BEYOND THE INTERNATIONAL STYLE

The authoritarian nature of the International Style, and the rapidity of its success, inevitably provoked a reaction. This reaction varied in character, from expressionist to a revival of classical features, but it was universally characterized by a rejection of the uniformity and purism of the Miesian style. Following the example of Alvar Aalto and Le Corbusier, many of the architects involved had been practitioners of the International Style and rejected it. Others, notably Frank Lloyd Wright, had consistently remained outside the movement.

Wright's work before World War I had been recognized by the architects of the International Style as seminal to their own development. It is indicative of his greatness that Wright's architectural style remained independent from the modern movement and continued to develop throughout. His rejection of the International Style had been apparent in the late 1930s, when he began to experiment with noncubic forms, such as the circle, and he continued to use rounded forms in his postwar architecture. His most famous building from this period is the Guggenheim Museum, New York (designed 1943-6; built 1956-9). It was opened in October 1959 to very mixed reviews, five months after Wright's death. The building was meant to house a collection of nonrepresentational art and dispenses with traditional layout and forms. Closed rooms have been replaced by a single pedestrian ramp which curves around the central space in ever-increasing circles, constructed in smooth concrete and entirely unadorned. Although the helix is not expressed on the outside of the building, Wright suggests the form of the interior by constructing the exterior from four broad, superimposed circles that increase in diameter as they rise. Unlike Wright's other buildings, the Guggenheim Museum does not relate to its surroundings. On the contrary, it makes a deliberate statement by contrasting with the commercial blocks around it.

Wright continued his experiments with the circle, and its more dynamic relation, the helix. The V C Morris Gift Shop, San Francisco (1948-9), was his first completed building to incorporate the spiraling form of the interior of the Guggenheim. The façade of the building is deceptively plain, with a simple rounded entrance arch. In contrast, the interior has a broad ramp, which spirals up the side of the walls. Wright also used the circle as the basic unit for a number of his private houses from the postwar period. The second Herbert Jacobs House, Middleton, Wisconsin (1948), consists of a two-story block, shaped in a semicircle, with the other half of the circle forming the garden, showing a typical Wrightian solution to the problem of integrating the building with its surroundings. His Sol Friedman House, Pleasantville, New York (1948-9), is roofed with circular slabs of concrete and its plan is based on two intersecting circles. The rough texture of its heavy masonry structure is also an important feature of the house he built for his son David, near Phoenix, Arizona (1952). The

**Above:** Wright, Johnson Wax Co Tower, Racine, Wisconsin, 1947-50. Built to house laboratories, this tower expands slightly as it rises, in direct criticism of the geometrical purity of the International Style.

**Left:** Wright, Beth Sholom Synagogue, Elkins Park, Pennsylvania, 1959. This synagogue typifies the formalism of his later works, with its emphasis on the triangle.

**Right:** Wright, Guggenheim Museum, New York City, 1943-59. Curved forms contrast with the angularity of the International Style, showing Wright's insistence on individual creativity.

**Below:** Wright, Guggenheim Museum, New York City, 1943-59. Experiments with the helix produced this original pedestrian viewing ramp.

David Wright House is built on thick, trunklike stilts, with a circle of rooms grouped around a central space. Unlike the Guggenheim, this central space is closed off from the house for practical reasons, but the Guggenheim helix features in the gently spiraling ramp, through which the building is reached, and the furniture Wright designed for the house echoes its circular form.

In 1947 he began a second phase of building for the Johnson Wax Company, designing a tower with an office block which connected to

**Above:** Saarinen, Dulles Airport Terminal Building, Chantilly, Virginia, 1958-62. An attempt to achieve monumentality through the expressive use of form.

Wright's earlier Administration Building. The tower follows the rounded form of the Administration Building and is constructed largely of brick and glass. Inside the tower are the laboratories, which are cantilevered out from a central core containing the lift. At ground level the surrounding courtyard extends into the building, under the cantilevered floors to this central core. In order to make the tower more impressive, Wright expanded it slightly as it rose, a clear criticism of the geometrical purity of the International Style. Wright's later projects show a preference for rounded forms above all others, and they lack the power and imagination of his earlier designs, degenerating into formalism. His Marin County Civic Center, San Rafael, California (1959-64), spreads out across the site in the manner of many of his earlier works, but it shows an exotic and fantastic tendency in its ornate and decorative features, which have none of the boldness and grandeur of the Robie House or Taliesin West.

The early works of Eero Saarinen conform to the Miesian purity of form. He came to the United States in 1923 with his parents and, after a traditional architectural education at Yale, went into partnership with his father. Eliel Saarinen had practiced as an architect in Finland, designing the railroad Station in Helsinki (1904) in a simplified neoclassical style, and his buildings in the United States combined classical forms with the use of vernacular materials. Eero went into partnership with his father in 1937 and they won a competition for an extension to the Smithsonian Museum, Washington DC (1939). Their major joint venture was the Lutheran Church of Christ, Minneapolis, Minnesota (1949-50), which was designed to be built on a very small budget and is thus of necessity extremely simple. The main body of the church has a flat roof which slopes down at the back and it is flanked by a simple bell tower. The church and tower are made of brick, handled in a simple and rational way, very much in the Scandinavian vernacular tradition. Eero Saarinen's General Motors Technical Center, Warren, Michigan (1949-55), follows the metal-and-glass structure of the International Style, appropriately for an industrial complex.

In his later buildings Saarinen rejected the rectilinearity of the International Style in favor of a much more sculptural and expressive approach. His Chapel at Massachusetts Institute of Technology (MIT), Cambridge, Massachusetts (1952-4), is a circular brick building, whose austerity is enlivened by low arches around the base. Designed just after Mies van der Rohe's IIT chapel, it can be seen as a direct critique of Mies' steel-and-glass cubic box. Saarinen's experiments with curved forms and his use of brick suggest the influence of Alvar Aalto, who had rejected the International Style. The curved forms of Aalto's Finnish Pavilion, New York World's Fair (1939) and his use of brick for a dormitory block at MIT, Baker House (1947-8), showed an alternative approach to the steel-and-glass rectilinearity of the International Style.

Saarinen's TWA Terminal, Kennedy Airport, New York (1956-62) shows just how far he had moved from the functional style of his earlier General Motors complex. Instead of the efficient and impersonal, but faceless, image, Saarinen used curved concrete forms deliber-

ately to give drama to the building and to suggest, appropriately, a bird in flight. Inside, the space is dynamic, with flowing forms and a variety of differing vistas, but he retained an awareness of purpose and the building functions well. It is a long way from the ascetic purity of the International Style. Saarinen started to experiment with concrete to produce more expressive forms. He had judged the Sydney Opera House competition in 1956 and was clearly influenced by the interesting shapes of the concrete shells in the winning design by Jørn Utzon and by the postwar buildings of Le Corbusier. The success of the TWA Terminal led to a Federal Government commission to design the Dulles Airport Terminal Building, Chantilly, Va (1958-62). In this building Saarinen created a more delicate structure with an upward-curving roof, again suggestive of flight. These experiments with the expressive potential of concrete also resulted in the fish-shape of the Ingalls Ice Hockey Rink, Yale, New Haven, Connecticut (1956-8). Saarinen's office was an important training ground for architects, such as Cesar Pelli, Kevin Roche and John Dinkeloo, and his expressive and dramatic style was an important influence on later developments.

Paul Rudolph's experiments in the use of concrete also mark his rejection of the International Style. His early buildings are indicative of his training under Gropius and Breuer at Harvard, but his dissatisfaction with the Miesian box led to designs that deliberately broke up the simple lines of modernism. He was

**Above:** Saarinen, MIT Chapel, Cambridge, Massachusetts, 1952-4. His choice of round forms and brick construction can be seen as a direct criticism of the Miesian box.

**Right:** Saarinen, TWA Terminal, John F Kennedy Airport, New York City, 1956-62. The image of flight is entirely appropriate and the building functions well too.

**Left:** Saarinen, Morse College, Yale University, New Haven, Connecticut, 1960-2. Saarinen's experiments with form provide an important influence on more recent developments in architecture.

appointed head of the Yale School of Architecture in 1958 and began work on the new building to house his department in the same year. In contrast to the simplicity of Mies' Crown Hall, the architectural department at IIT, the Yale building, is highly complex and sculptural, following Le Corbusier in its expression of chaos rather than the Miesian imposition of

**Below:** Rudolph, Walker Guest House, Sanibel Island, Florida, 1952-3. A technological version of the Glass Box, with an emphasis on function, rather than luxury.

**Right:** Rudolph, Yale Art & Architecture Building, New Haven, Connecticut, 1963. Complex and sculptural, this building provides a dramatic contrast with the geometrical purity of Mies' IIT buildings.

**Right:** Becket, Capitol Records Building, Los Angeles, California, 1954: a stack of records and an appropriate image for the music business.

rational order. There are over 30 different floor levels, within a mass of interrelated and interpenetrating blocks of very heavily textured concrete, reminiscent of De Stijl designs. This emphasis on formal confusion reached its peak in Rudolph's project for the Graphic Arts Center, New York (1967), with its futuristic towers composed of hundreds of angular blocks jutting out from a central core.

In contrast to the aggressive character of Rudolph's designs, Minoru Yamasaki and Edward Durrell Stone developed elaborately elegant and decorative styles based on the use of concrete. Yamasaki's McGregor Memorial Conference Center, Wayne State University, Detroit, Michigan (1958), sits beside a water garden, a reflection of his Japanese background. The façade and interior hall are decorated with a pattern of projecting diamonds, which are reflected in the detailing of the glass roof. This highly decorative approach to design is also evident in the elegant articulation of the cubic box for the Harvard Engineering Sciences Building, Cambridge, Massachusetts (1962). Traditional Arabian motifs were the inspiration for the form of the concrete structure of Dharan Airport, Saudi Arabia (1961). Its intersecting pointed arches and tracery patterns show an emphasis on decoration, which was a conscious revival of ideals forcefully rejected by the International Style.

A similar revival of the decorative qualities

of earlier architecture is apparent in the later works of Stone, who, together with Philip Goodwin, had designed one of the earliest public buildings of the International Style in New York, the Museum of Modern Art (1939). His later buildings show a marked reaction in favor of an elegant and decorative approach. The Huntingdon-Hartford Gallery of Modern Art, New York (1964-5) showed Stone's dissatisfaction with the austerity of the International Style with its pierced decoration and the transformation of *pilotis* into elegant arches. His United States Embassy, New Delhi (1958) revived the prewar preference for classical styles to convey the image of the state, its rectangular colonnaded form based on Ancient Greek temples. The building has elegant, gilded columns and Stone pierced the walls behind with an intricate and detailed pattern, preferring a light, frivolous interpretation to the simple austerity of prewar classicism. Philip Johnson also rejected Miesian purity in favor of classical forms in the façades of the New York Theater in the Lincoln Center (1960-4) and the Sheldon Art Gallery, Lincoln, Nebraska (1963). The Sheldon Art Gallery, in particular, emphasizes the purely decorative nature of this revival, with its tapering piers and its lack of concern for structural honesty.

In the area of domestic architecture, the works of Bruce Goff and Herbert Greene also illustrate the rejection of the International Style and the search for different sources of inspiration. Goff was much influenced by Wright's spatial experiments, and he took the triangle as the basic unit for the Triaer Vacation House, Fern Creek, Louisville, Kentucky (1940-1). The triangle is expressed in the plan as well as in the extraordinary forms of the ex-

**Above:** Stone, Kennedy Center, Washington DC, 1964-71. A modern temple to culture? It has none of the grandeur of original Greek temples.

**Left:** Stone, Kennedy Center, Washington DC, 1964-71. Frivolity and wealth are expressed in the thin, gilded columns which support the roof.

**Right:** Fuller, Geodesic Dome, Montreal, Canada. A system of construction based on octahedrons, developed as a practical solution to the problem of enclosing large areas.

**Below:** Fuller, Repair shop, Union Tank Car Co, Baton Rouge, Louisiana, 1958. Practical, functional and new but without the intellectual conformity required by the modern movement.

terior, with its roof soaring upward and outward like a pair of wings. In the Ford Residence, Aurora, Illinois (1949), Goff used more curvaceous shapes and, although the flat domes have an eastern exoticism about them, his style is hardly revivalist. The Bavinger House, Norman, Oklahoma (1951-5), with its spiraling roof and unusual curved walls, shows Goff's concern for volume. The materials he used for his houses, which included rubble from local fields, anthracite and oil pipes, show a markedly nonconformist attitude to modern

structural methods. The houses of Herbert Greene are even more extraordinary. His own house at Norman, Oklahoma (1960-1) shows the influence of Goff, whom he much admired, developing a similar preoccupation with form. The house is hardly recognizable as such, looking like a bird-shaped collection of junk, but on closer inspection the building is carefully constructed to convey this impression of unreality. The domestic architecture of Paolo Soleri was based on a more functional approach to house design, without the extreme formalism of Goff and Greene. Soleri's Desert House, Cave Creek, Arizona (1951-2), designed in collaboration with Mark Mills, is set into the ground and has a domed glass roof which can be retracted when necessary.

Buckminster Fuller's rejection of the International Style and his experiments in technological innovation continued after the war. His Dymaxion House (1927) was followed by the development of his 'Geodesic Domes.' These structures, which could be made out of a variety of materials, were based on octahedrons or tetrahedrons. They were developed more for their efficiency as a lightweight means of enclosing space than for their formal symbolism. His most famous dome was designed for the United States Pavilion at Expo '67, Montreal (1967), but his largest was for the repair shop of the Union Tank Car Company, Baton Rouge, Louisiana (1958), which had a diameter of 384 feet. More recently he has experimented with 'Tensegrity Structures' ('tensional' plus 'integrity'), in an attempt to improve on the size, strength and lightness of his large-scale buildings. Fuller's technological approach to the design of a controlled environment experimented with ways in which man could relate to nature through the machine. The boldness and novelty of his designs made them less acceptable to the convention-bound public, and this has been reflected in a lack of commissions. Fuller's influence has been through his teaching and it is only recently, with the growing change in attitudes toward architecture and design, that his ideas are beginning to get the attention they deserve.

## MONUMENTALITY AND THE LURE OF CLASSICISM

The issue of monumentality was a problem for the architects of the modern movement. The International Style, in its pursuit of antihistoricism, had deliberately sought images that were not monumental. Monumentality had been the major preoccupation of the reaction to the International Style in the neoclassical imagery of Hitler, Stalin and Mussolini. The need for monumentality, to produce monuments which outlived their own period and became the heritage of future generations, was recognized by Sigfried Giedion and José Luis Sert in their *Nine Points on Monumentality* (1943). They also recognized the necessity of finding new ways of expressing it. However,

**Below:** Mies van der Rohe, New National Gallery of Art, Berlin, Germany, 1963. Attempts to achieve monumentality with the International Style proved to be unsuccessful.

the architecture of the International Style lacks the intrinsic qualities needed for such survival. The association of the thinness, lightness and vulnerability of steel-and-glass structures with disposability and the built-in obsolescence of commerce makes this style inadequate for the monumental images required by society. Its use suggests a fear to put trust in tradition. Monumentality is a concept associated with mass, solidity, weight and immovability and, inevitably, with the classical tradition. The monuments of Greece and Rome survived the tests of time and the fundamental changes of the Middle Ages. The problems of conveying the monumental essence of classical architecture in a modern idiom meant a break with the International Style.

Le Corbusier was one of the few architects to achieve this. Inspired by the spirit of classical architecture, his use of expressive concrete forms showed how monumentality could be achieved without the use of overt classical imagery. However, the belief that classical style was the best means of conveying monumentality persisted, notably in the state images of Saarinen's United States Embassy, London (1955-60), and Stone's United States Embassy, New Delhi (1958). Stone's Embassy, in particular, shows a superficial and decorative use of classically inspired details but it lacks an understanding of the spirit of classical architecture and fails to achieve the monumentality to which it aspired. Equally unsuccessful attempts resulted in Johnson's New York Theater (1960-4) and his Sheldon Art Gallery, Lincoln, Nebraska (1963). A more serious attempt to revive the monumentality of historical tradition in architecture was made by Kallmann, McKinnell and Knowles with the Boston City Hall, Mass (1964), but it was Kahn who really started to come to terms with the problem.

As early as 1943, Louis Kahn had questioned the ability of steel structures to convey monumentality in architecture because of their lack of weight. Kahn had graduated from the University of Pennsylvania in 1924, receiving a traditional Beaux-Arts training in architecture, but had done little when in 1950, he went to the American Academy in Rome, and traveled in Greece and Egypt. The importance of his classical training and travels became obvious when he rejected the steel and glass of the International Style, preferring heavier materials in his development of massive masonry walls, recalling the buildings of Ancient Rome and also the works of Le Corbusier, Aalto and Wright. His buildings show other allusions to Rome, such as formal grid plans and axial layouts, and arches supported by piers.

Kahn's lack of faith in the functional attitude to design of the International Style led him to develop a less definable, more mystical approach. He aimed to understand the essence of the building, which he called 'form,' and argued that design was both inspired by and grew naturally from an understanding of 'form.' He made a distinction between the main parts of the building and its services in terms of 'served' and 'servant,' reflected in his complex gridded layouts around a central space.

**Right:** Kahn, Salk Institute, La Jolla, California, 1959-65. Kahn's work was the product of a highly intellectual approach to design, appropriate for an image of research and education.

**Above:** Kahn, Ahmadabad Institute of Management, India, 1964. Simple pierced shapes continue Mogul traditions, expressing Kahn's idea of the 'form' of a building.

The bulk of his commissions were for educational, cultural and research institutions where his intellectual approach to design was certainly appropriate. His first major work was an extension to the Yale Art Gallery, New Haven, Connecticut (1952-4). By contrasting blank concrete with steel and glass for the exterior walls of the gallery, Kahn displayed an independence from Miesian formal purity. This is also reflected in the more complex treatment of the open façade, with patterns of unequal glass panels through which the triangular grid pattern of the interior ceiling is a visible reference to the coffering of ancient Rome. In 1955 he was commissioned to design a Jewish Community Center in Trenton, New Jersey, but only the Bath House (1958) was completed. This project makes a clearer statement of intent. The solid square central block, with smaller square blocks at each of the four corners and crowned by a flattened pyramidal roof, has all the massivity, though none of the arches, of a Roman bath complex.

In 1955 Kahn was appointed Professor of Architecture at the University of Pennsylvania, Philadelphia, where he designed the Richards Medical Research Building (1958-60) as a series of laboratory units attached to massive brick towers, which house the service elements of the building and show how far he had moved from the International Style. Johnson's Kline Laboratory, Yale University, New Haven, Connecticut (1962-6), is similar in function and in its use of heavy materials, but Johnson's concern is with the appearance of the building, the monolithic image, rather than Kahn's 'form.' The commission for the Jonas Salk Institute for Biological Studies, La Jolla, California (1959-65), was more complicated, requiring not only research laboratories and studies, but also communal meeting areas and private living quarters. Kahn separated the three areas, designing a complex which reflected the varying degrees of privacy. The central feature was the laboratory buildings placed on either side of a vast 'avenue' directed over the Pacific to the horizon, combining the grandeur of classical architecture with the austerity of a monastery in an attempt to convey the 'form' of the institution.

Kahn's largest commission was for the planning of the government buildings at Dacca, Bangladesh (1962-76). This complex, which was completed after his death, provided him

with a truly monumental challenge. The buildings are planned around a central core, expressing the 'form' of the project, which consists of tall angular and rounded blocks grouped round a central circle housing the main chamber of the Assembly. These huge, solid blocks are constructed from masonry and pierced with circular, triangular and square openings, which are large and simple and quite unlike the fussy and delicate pierced detailing of Stone. These large openings refer to the pre-British imperial tradition of the Moguls and buildings such as the Taj Mahal, but their pointed arches have been replaced by the simpler shapes of ancient Rome. The simple and austere forms recall Muslim architecture and deliberately contrast with the more sculptural decoration of Hindu tradition. The buildings convey a complex range of values but, above all, stability and tradition. Kahn's architecture shows a genuine attempt to infuse modern forms with the spirit and the monumentality of the past. Acknowledging his debt to Le Corbusier and dissatisfied with the wholesale adoption of the International Style as a uniform for a building, Kahn aimed to create new and meaningful solutions to architectural problems in postwar America and his approach was extremely influential.

## THE RECONSTRUCTION OF EUROPE

The devastation left by the war in Europe was so extensive that it necessitated state intervention on an unprecedented scale. The immediate problem facing governments and their architects was the urgent provision of low-cost housing, the perfect opportunity to put into practice the ideals of the International Style developed before the war. The starting point for Gropius and the modern movement had been the design of state-financed low-cost housing projects for the poor. This had led to the development of standardization and prefabrication to provide uniform housing units, reflecting socialist equality and replacing the nineteenth-century slums, which had been the direct result of pursuing the capitalist profit motive. If the stylistic issues of the modern movement were paramount in the United

**Above:** Kahn, Yale Center for British Art, New Haven, Connecticut, 1969-74: an intellectual image and modern forms, suggesting the spirit of the past?

**Left:** Kahn, Kimbell Art Museum, Fort Worth, Texas, 1972. Simple forms, inspired by the architecture of classical Rome, also convey its monumentality.

**Right:** Candilis et al, Bagnols-sur-Cèze, France, 1956-60. Rigid functional zoning was dropped in the 1950s in favor of a more organic approach to town-planning.

**Below:** Van den Broek & Bakema, Lijnbaan Centre, Rotterdam, the Netherlands, 1951-3. This early shopping center and residential development were part of a project to revive the urban center after wartime devastation.

States, it was the social and industrial elements of the International Style that dominated post-war architecture in Europe. Commercial patronage dominated in the United States but state patronage set the pattern in Europe.

The radical idea that it was the moral duty of the state to provide low-cost housing was a key issue at the first meeting in 1928 of the *Congrès Internationaux d'Architecture Moderne* (CIAM), which also stressed the changing role of the architect from the artistic to the political and social arena. Later CIAM conferences had developed this community approach to building by encouraging governments to set up

state-financed urban development schemes based on their theories of town-planning which, under the influence of Le Corbusier, involved rigid functional zoning of cities, set in green belts, and urban housing in large apartment blocks. The 1953 CIAM conference saw the rejection of rigid zoning by the younger generation of architects in favor of a looser and more organic approach to planning. This group, known as Team X, included the Smithsons, van Eyck, Candilis and Bakema, and it had an important influence on the development of planning, based on Le Corbusier's commitment to International Style ideals.

In Britain, the election of a Labour Government in 1945 committed to social reform led to the nationalization of the coal, gas, transport and electricity industries and the setting up of the Welfare State in 1948. This reformist spirit was expressed architecturally in the adoption of the ideals of the International Style and CIAM. Wartime restrictions on private building were not lifted until 1954 and it was the state who commissioned the badly needed housing, new towns and schools. In 1946 Parliament passed the New Towns Act for the state financing of 12 new towns, which were planned as independent satellites to major conurbations, including Hatfield, Basildon and Bracknell around London, Peterlee in County Durham and Cwmbran in South Wales. They were designed as self-contained units, with a commercial and civic center serving the residential and industrial areas arranged around the center and limited in size, with a projected population that varied from 20,000 to 70,000. Following the theories of CIAM and Le Corbusier they were to be surrounded by green belts, an idea born in the English garden cities of the late-nineteenth century. Another important Corbusian feature was the bypassing of through traffic and the segregation of vehicular and pedestrian traffic in the town wherever possible. Although the planning was innovatory, most of the housing was built in traditional styles, but there were notable exceptions such as Fry and Drew's work at Harlow, which showed their preference for the prewar International Style.

The 1947 Town Planning Act dealt with the redevelopment of damaged city centers, like Coventry, which had been almost destroyed, encouraging local government authorities to provide urgently needed housing. High-rise blocks of flats were developed to solve the problem of growing demand and lack of space, a radical break from the English tradition of individual dwelling units. Scotland, with its strong historical links with mainland Europe, had developed the apartment block much earlier. These high-rise blocks appealed to the architect, who felt he was realizing the aims of

**Below:** Safdie et al, Habitat, Expo '67, Montreal, Canada, 1967. Experiments with open and closed space led to new solutions for the problem of urban housing.

CIAM and the prewar leaders such as Le Corbusier and Gropius. They appealed to the local authorities at a more practical level, with standardization and prefabrication producing a quick and cheap solution to their problems. The Alton West Estate, Roehampton, London (1955-9), was designed by the Architects' Department of the London County Council (LCC) and it is typical of the LCC's housing projects of the 1950s. The estate was intended to house 10,000 people in ten- and six-story blocks with four-story terraces, set in lawns beside Richmond Park. The six-story blocks were cheap imitations of Le Corbusier's Unité d'Habitation and other Corbusian features included the use of *pilotis* to support the taller tower blocks. Later developments moved away from the rigid layout of the Roehampton Estate in an attempt to encourage a 'sense of belonging.' Alison and Peter Smithson, leading members of Team X, criticized the rigid functional zoning of the CIAM model and proposed a more organic development. Their Golden Lane project (1952) attempted to provide an architectural formula that would re-create the community atmosphere of the old slums, and they abandoned the isolated block in favor of longer units arranged around spaces. A similar approach inspired Lynn and Smith's Park Hill Estate, Sheffield (1961), with its angular blocks curving in a layout based on function and responding to the topography of the site.

Major advances in standardization and prefabrication were made in postwar Britain. A sudden and urgent need for more schools was created by the 1948 Education Act, which raised the school-leaving age to 15, and by a general population shift from city centers to the suburbs. This demand, combined with a shortage of skilled labor and supplies, encouraged the County Architect of Hertfordshire, C H Aslin, to develop a system of flexible prefabrication, using standardized parts such as walls and roofing, which could be assembled cheaply and easily in a variety of ways. Aslin's approach was immediately influential and other similar schemes followed. CLASP (the Consortium of Local Authorities Special Programme) was set up in 1957 by a group of local authorities. Their design won the gold medal at the Milan Triennale, 1960. The CLASP system was taken up in West Germany and Italy and stimulated the development of similar systems in France and the United States, thus finally realizing one of the ideals of the modern movement on the international scale envisaged by Gropius in the 1920s.

In France the necessity for postwar rebuilding was recognized by the setting up of a Ministry of Reconstruction and Town-Planning in 1944, which led to Perret's appointment as head of the team rebuilding the Channel port of Le Havre, and Le Corbusier's projects for La Rochelle-Pallice and Saint-Dié. In 1948 the urgent demand for housing resulted in a state-financed policy of building large urban residential complexes, *grands ensembles*, with over 1000 apartments. The scale of industrialized building in France was unparalleled. As in England, there was an initial compromise between the urgency of the short-term need for housing and the necessity for long-term planning. By the mid-1950s the influence of Le Corbusier's ideas, which had shaped the attitudes of the younger generation of architects in their approach to design, was noticeable. Georges Candilis, who had emigrated from Russia in 1945, joined Le Corbusier's office and worked on the Unité d'Habitation in Marseilles. In collaboration with Josic and Woods, he planned the layout of a number of towns following the Team X critique of the CIAM model. Toulouse-le-Mirail (begun 1960) provided housing for 10,000 in blocks of varying heights and standard social services and amenities, with the Corbusian separation of high-speed traffic from local vehicular and pedestrian routes. Another of their projects, Bagnols-sur-Cèze (1956-60), involved the collaboration of Jean Prouvé, whose development of the curtain wall in the 1930s had resulted in his specialization of standardized and prefabricated building units. Other architects developed less rectilinear styles, such as Emile Aillaud's serpentine composition of his residential blocks for the Les Courtillières housing estate, Pantin (1955-60), in an attempt to encourage inhabitants to identify with their environment.

Holland already possessed a tradition of high-quality housing schemes established by Oud, de Klerk and Kramer in the 1920s, and this continued. One of the most important schemes was the realization of prewar plans for reclaiming land in the North Sea, which increased the quantity of available land for habitation. The ideals of the International Style were already well established and the Dutch architects made better use of their limited funds than the British and French. The development of the Lijnbaan Centre, Rotterdam (1951-3), by Jacob van den Broek and Jacob B Bakema included a shopping area and residential blocks. Their concern for the inhabitants showed in attention to details like benches, shelters and plants. The long shopping street is flanked by housing in a variety of multistory blocks set in ample green spaces. Van den Broek and Bakema were involved in other planning projects, including further work in Rotterdam, a major proposal for the extension of Amsterdam and the building of Nagele on the Noordostpolder, which was reclaimed between 1937 and 1942. On a smaller scale, Aldo van Eyck's Municipal Orphanage, Amsterdam (1957-60), deliberately suggests intimacy and security by the use of small units and the very

**Left:** London County Council, Alton West Estate, Roehampton, London, 1955-9. Designed according to Le Corbusier's principles, this low-cost housing estate has become the symbol of the failure of the modern movement to provide an attractive environment to live in.

private bedrooms over glazed recreation areas. The irregularity of the layout of the complex lacks the imposed order of the International Style and shows a sensitive understanding of the function of the building. Van Eyck's work shows how far advanced Holland was in the development of the concept of designing for people rather than strict adherence to a set of idealized rules.

In general Scandinavia maintained its pre-war tradition of excellence with much comfortable and well-designed housing and community schemes. Sweden devoted great care to the development of its city centers and suburbs. Vallingby, near Stockholm, designed by Stockholm's chief architect, Sven Markelius (begun 1953), was planned as a residential suburb, set in trees and parkland, with recreational and cultural facilities and good communications with Stockholm. Finland developed the concept of the garden city with Tapiola (begun 1953), the center by Arne Ervi (1954-69) reflecting Le Corbusier's urban designs. A strong vernacular tradition and less urgent demand for housing in postwar Scandinavia has led to a more humanitarian approach to design and a greater concentration on long-term planning.

The situation in Germany was very different. The scale of the wartime devastation meant that the urgent need for housing took precedence over long-term planning. In many cities, notably Berlin and Cologne, over 70 percent of the center had been destroyed and in 1948 over 6,000,000 houses were needed. The closure of the Bauhaus in 1933 had abruptly terminated the tradition of experimental thought and the emigration of most of the major prewar architects left few trained to deal effectively with the reconstruction. One of these was Max Taut, the brother of Bruno, who designed housing estates in Bonn (1949-52), Berlin (1954), and Duisburg (1955-64). Another was Hans Scharoun who was made Director of Building and Housing in Berlin after the war. His so-called 'Romeo and Julia' apartment block in Stuttgart (1954-9) continued the expressionist style of his earlier works, with a marked tendency away from the curving forms of his prewar buildings toward more angular and aggressive shapes. The ground plan of the Julia block consists of a series of protruding triangular units arranged in a horseshoe, which rise to heights ranging from five to 12 stories, emphasizing the angularity of the design.

In 1957 the Berlin Senate arranged the Interbau Exhibition in Charlottenburg to contribute to the rebuilding of the Hansa quarter which had been almost totally destroyed. Many important architects were involved, including Le Corbusier, Aalto, Niemeyer and Gropius, whose housing block was designed with Wils Ebert. Gropius also designed the layout of the new town of Britz-Buckow-Rudow. The Interbau exhibition attempted to re-create the prewar eminence of architecture in Germany, in imitation of the Weissenhof exhibition in Stuttgart (1927), but despite the quality of the contributors it never achieved the standard of its predecessors. The same desire led to the setting up of a new Bauhaus in 1955, housed in the Hochschule für Gestaltung (College of Design) in Ulm, designed by Max Bill (1954-5), a student at the original Bauhaus. The simple blocks were built from prefabricated units in imitation of Gropius' complex at Dessau. However, the bulk of the housing projects undertaken after the war consisted of huge complexes of high-rise blocks sited on the edge of cities, such as the Märkisches Viertel housing estate, Berlin (1962-72) by Müller, Heinrichs and Düttmann, which fulfilled urgent needs but lacked planning and contributed nothing to the quality of life in postwar Germany.

Similar problems faced Italy, with serious war damage and a major population shift into the cities. In 1949 the government decided on a deliberate policy of constructing low-cost housing to solve the two problems of unemployment and housing shortage in the cities by building new workers' housing blocks on the city boundaries. However, the lack of serious planning or social commitment on the part of the successive right-wing Christian Democratic governments gave rise to corruption and a lot of badly designed high-rise blocks which conformed only vaguely to building codes. Architectural innovation was limited to commercial and private patronage. The enlightened attitude of patrons such as Adriano Olivetti led to the commissioning of Olivetti complexes at Ivrea (1947-57) by Luigi Figini and Gino Pollini, and at Pozzuoli (1954) by Luigi Cosenza, which included offices and industrial buildings as well as housing for the workforces and amenities such as a school and social center. However, it was not until the late 1960s when widespread social disorder threatened revolution that the state intervened and major advances in the design of low-cost housing were made.

The Italian experience was more dramatic but, with the notable exceptions of Holland and Scandinavia, the same pattern is discernible in the rest of Europe. Initial enthusiasm was followed by a growing lack of ideological commitment on the part of authorities responsible for the provision of low-cost housing and a marked laxity in enforcing building regulations to save money. These factors, together with an adherence to the stylistic rules of the modern movement and a lack of realistic humanitarian concern on the part of the architectural profession, led to stagnation and, on occasion, to disaster.

## EUROPEAN REACTIONS TO THE INTERNATIONAL STYLE

European architecture after the war had less of the material enthusiasm so evident in the United States. Lack of private patronage, the channeling of available funds into essential reconstruction, and the experimental vacuum left by the departure of the modern movement for the United States; all combined to create an atmosphere in which the prewar ideals of the International Style flourished but its postwar forms did not. As Europe came to terms with the devastation of war, innovation and experimentation began slowly to develop. Le Corbusier's postwar rejection of the International Style was a formative influence on many of the younger generation of architects, stimulating a variety of different approaches to the problem of design.

In Scandinavia there was a mixed reaction to the International Style. Arne Jacobsen, under the influence of Mies van der Rohe, infused industrial design with an extreme elegance in the Town Hall, Rødovre, Copenhagen (1954-6), with its steel-skeleton structure encased in concrete and completely hidden behind the sheer glass curtain walls of the exterior, very similar to the geometrical purity and structure of Mies van der Rohe. Other architects were profoundly influenced by the works of Alvar Aalto, who had abandoned the purism of the International Style in the 1930s and developed his own personal style. Aalto approached the problem of design with a belief that human architecture was better architecture and that technical and stylistic considerations were not paramount. He rejected the rectilinear industrial style of the modern movement, preferring to use traditional materials, notably wood and brick, thus introducing variety into the forms of his buildings and concentrating on practicality and comfort. Through occasional teaching posts at MIT, he was commissioned to design a block of student residences, Baker House, MIT, Cambridge, Massachusetts (1946-8). In deliberate contrast to the new Miesian mood of American architecture, Aalto designed a serpentine block constructed in heavily textured red brick. The curved form, which allowed variety in room shapes and also in their views of the Charles River beyond, was chosen for practical and humane reasons rather than as an experiment with the shape itself. Not surprisingly, it had little influence in the United States.

Aalto also used brick for the Civic Center, Säynätsalo (1949-52). It is one of a series of complexes showing his ingenuity in grouping buildings round focal points in order to achieve a human scale, unlike the faceless images of the International Style or the deliberate grandeur of Kahn. The Säynätsalo complex suggests natural growth rather than imposed order in a series of changes in level, small irregular spaces and a variety of angular forms. The rapid ageing of the brick has given the complex a sense of permanence. There are no vast open spaces to awe the user and the constant changes of direction are reminiscent of medieval alleys. The complex includes the Council Chamber as well as the Public Library, offices and shops, organized around an elevated courtyard. The library is separate, facing the U-shaped group across the square and the whole has a remarkably natural homogeneity,

**Below:** Aalto, Säynätsalo Civic Center, Finland, 1949-52. The rapid ageing of the brick has given this complex a feeling of permanency and security, lacking in many modern developments.

partly the result of the textured brick walls that unify the diverse forms of the roofline. Aalto's ability to compose unified groups of unusual shapes found further expression in the Otaiemi Institute of Technology (1955-64), which consists of groups of rectangular teaching and administration blocks with a fan-shaped lecture theater that acts as a central pivot. Curtis *(Modern Architecture since 1900)* has pointed out that Aalto's use of the fan shape as the pivotal point of a complex of buildings probably derives from his studies of Ancient Greek architecture, notably Delphi, and the series of forms that center around the theater. This theme occurs again in his design for the Wolfsburg Cultural Center, West Germany (1959-62) with its series of lecture theaters fanning out on one side of the complex.

Aalto's preference for brick was not restrictive. His ability to use other materials is displayed in the marble facing of the courtyard of the Rautatalo (Steel Federation) Building, Helsinki (1952-3), and the rendered white walls of his Maison Carré, Bazoches-sur-Guyonne, France (1956-8). This rectilinear and extensively glazed villa recalls the International Style, but Aalto criticizes its formal purity with his complicated plan and dominant sloping roof. He also used white rendered surfaces in the Vuoksenniska Church, Imatra (1956-8), which was intended as a community center as well as a place of worship. The building can be separated into three parts by means of movable and sound-proofed concrete screens, and these three sections are recognizable on the exterior by separate, but interlocking, units composed of curved and straight lines. This mixture of forms, typical of Aalto, is also evident in the interior and, although potentially chaotic, Aalto's control of the design gives it a remarkable degree of unity. Like Le Corbusier, Aalto aimed not to impose form but to let his forms reflect the untidyness of human nature. His architecture is expressive, subtly conveying a series of messages through spatial complexity. Although influenced by the modern movement, he rejected the authoritarian forms of the International Style, showing a deliberate concern for the use of a building and a style strongly rooted in tradition.

Another Scandinavian architect to develop away from the International Style was Jørn Utzon. Deeply influenced by Aalto, with whom he worked for part of 1946, Utzon visited Wright in the United States, developing an interest in his organic style. His experiments with spatial layouts resulted in interesting schemes for housing projects at Elsinore

**Left:** Aalto, Finlandia Hall, Helsinki, Finland, 1955-8. A rich variety of forms shows Aalto's independence from the International Style.

**Below:** Nervi & Vitelozzi, Palazetto dello Sport, Rome, Italy, 1956-7. This exciting and original structure covers space for 5000 spectators.

**Above:** Utzon, Sydney Opera House, Australia, 1956-73. Despite their initial unpopularity, these bizarre concrete shells have become the image of modern Australia.

**Below:** Montuori, Catini et al, Rome Termini Station, Italy, 1947-51. The power of concrete is expressed in this huge vault, which spans the station entrance hall, creating a dramatic effect.

(1956-60) and Fredensborg (1962-3), but his masterpiece was the Opera House, Sydney, Australia (1956-73). Apart from the Opera House itself, the complex included a theater, exhibition hall, cinema and other auditoria. It is one of the best-publicized and most controversial images of modern architecture, partly for its unorthodox style but mainly because of the cost, estimated at $7,000,000 in 1960 and completed for $100,000,000. Utzon resigned in 1966 after economic considerations entailed major changes in the design of the interior but it is his exterior concrete shells that give the building its individualism.

Dutch architects were mainly involved with the problems of reconstruction, developing an approach to design that concentrated on a humanization of the ideals of the International Style, particularly through the magazine *Forum*, edited by van Eyck, Bakema and Herman Hertzberger. Architects such as Rietveld continued to follow the industrial style of the modern movement in the Academy of Art, Arnhem (1962), and the Van Gogh Museum, Amsterdam (1963-72), but van Eyck and others developed a concern for individual needs. Van Eyck's Arnhem Pavilion (1964-6), displays sculpture in a series of small angular and rounded areas, which open into each other like a maze. His attitude to design owes much to Bauhaus idealism but it is based on an imaginative and small-scale approach to the concept of form following function.

In Italy major achievements were made in the use of concrete. Morandi's experiments in prestressed concrete produced stunning motorway viaducts, notably over the Torrente Polcevera, Genoa (1967). Another spectacular building was the main railroad station in Rome (1947-51), designed by a consortium of architects including Eugenio Montuori, Annibale Vitelozzi and the engineer Leo Catini. However, the Italian master of concrete was Nervi, who continued his prewar exploitation of its potential. His structures displayed imagination and originality in a style that was not historical, nor did it conform to the tenets of the International Style but derived from the material itself. His commissions were for large-scale buildings, mainly exhibition halls and sports stadia, where wide uninterrupted space was required and speed of construction was important. His Exhibition Hall, Turin (1948-9) was relatively simple, with an undulating roof made up of prefabricated units, but the sports halls for the Rome Olympics (1960) show a more imaginative approach to design. The Palazetto dello Sport (1956-7), designed with Vitelozzi has a circular shell roof supported by 36 Y-shaped units splaying out on to a concrete base. The Palazzo dello Sport (1958-60), designed with Piacentini, with a diameter of 328 feet and built to hold 16,000 spectators, is crowned with a hemispherical dome supported on diagonal posts. Nervi's skill led to his appointment as structural engineer on many prestigious projects, notably the UNESCO Building in Paris (1953-7) and the Pirelli Building, Milan (1955-9), which was designed with Gio Ponti. The Pirelli Building is one of the earliest European skyscrapers, its tapered outline breaking with the rectangular block of American tradition.

**Left:** Nervi & Ponti, Pirelli Building, Milan, Italy, 1955-9. Elegant and tapered, this reinforced-concrete skyscraper shows independence from the Miesian geometric box.

Another reinforced-concrete skyscraper in Milan, the Torre Velasca (1956-7), designed by the BBPR partnership, illustrates the shift toward historicism in Italian architecture of the late 1950s. The building has a projecting upper section, which distinguishes the apartments from the offices below, and an irregular window pattern in marked contrast to the normal standardized window module. It has more in common with the towers of medieval Italian cities than with the regular steel-and-glass boxes of the International Style. The importance of tradition in Italy is evident in the works of architects like Ignazio Gardella and Giancarlo de Carlo. Gardella's house on the Zattere, Venice (1957), reflects the style of Venetian Renaissance palaces interpreted in a modern idiom, and the same is true of his later works in Alessandria. De Carlo's designs for the university at Urbino (1962 onward) make interesting references to the traditional architecture of the city.

The relatively high standard of industrial design in Italy is partly due to the enlightened attitude of patrons like Adriano Olivetti, discussed above. Palazzo Olivetti (1954-5), designed by G A Bernasconi, Annibale Fiocchi and Marco Nizzoli as Olivetti's headquarters in Milan, shows the influence of Le Corbusier and combines *brise-soleil* and plain glass façades supported on *pilotis*. This functional and clean design was recognized at the São Paolo Biennale (1957) and was the only non-Brazilian building to be praised. Gino Valle's administration building for Rex Zanussi, Pordenone (1961), conforms more closely with the International Style but his irregular articulation of the concrete-and-glass façade demonstrates his independence.

Architecture outside Scandinavia, Holland and Italy did not reach the same high standards. When the competition for the UNESCO Building in Paris was announced in 1952, the panel of judges included Gropius, Costa, Le Corbusier, a Swede, Markelius, and

**Below:** Bernasconi, Fiocchi & Nizzoli, Palazzo Olivetti, Milan, Italy, 1954-5. Enlightened patrons, like Adriano Olivetti, encouraged the development of modern architecture in Italy.

**Above:** Spence, Coventry Cathedral, England, 1951-63. After the Gothic cathedral was destroyed by wartime bombs, the new cathedral was designed as a symbol of peace.

an Italian, Ernesto Rogers. The winning design was by a Frenchman, Bernard Zehrfuss, together with Marcel Breuer and with Nervi as structural engineer. The complex consists of a Secretariat and a concert hall. The latter, designed by Nervi with dramatic use of concrete beams, contrasts with the more detailed eight-story Secretariat with its *brise-soleil* façade and tapered columns.

The dramatic revival of the German economy in the 1950s resulted in many office blocks, mainly based on American prototypes. The partnership of Hentrich and Petschnigg in Germany occupied a similar position to that of SOM in the United States, and produced designs in the formal Miesian style beloved by modern corporations. Their BASF Building, Ludwigshafen (1958), was notable for its height, and the formal simplicity of the Phoenix-Rheinrohr Building, Düsseldorf (1957-60), is typical of the International Style in Europe. The most exciting work in Germany was done by Hans Scharoun, who developed the Expressionism of his prewar style. His project for a theater at Kassel (1952-3) was structurally daring and was not built, as the client feared that extra costs might be incurred by structural problems. In the Primary School, Marl (1960-8), Scharoun created a dynamic complex of interrelated shapes, quite unlike the static and simplified prefabricated school design more common in Germany and pioneered in Britain. His postwar masterpiece was the Berlin Philharmonic Concert Hall (1960-3), which follows the structural daring of the Kassel theater project. This is perhaps his most Expressionist building, with an irregular and apparently haphazard collection of individual elements convincingly ordered. Scharoun's imaginative approach stands out from the blandness of the rest of the German postwar architecture.

The buildings of postwar Britain show how profoundly architecture expresses the culture that creates it. Although the war had been won, rationing continued into the 1950s, the state took control of the major industries, and international power and prestige faded with the loss of the Empire. Due to restrictions on private patronage, architecture was dominated by state projects, largely housing and education. The ideals of the modern movement were eagerly pursued, but the International Style as interpreted by the masters now in the United States was avoided. The Festival of Britain was a deliberate, and characteristically half-

hearted, attempt to enliven the drabness of postwar Britain, to celebrate the centenary of the Great Exhibition of 1851, and the vanished imperial past. Stylistically it represented an equally half-hearted official acceptance of the modern architectural style in Britain and was derided by the younger generation of architects for being Swedish rather than modern. The Royal Festival Hall by the LCC architects Robert Matthew and Leslie Martin, made significant technical achievements in its acoustics, but the style of the building was typical of the Scandinavian-inspired official architecture of the Welfare State.

**Above:** A & P Smithson, Hunstanton School, Norfolk, England, 1949-54. Brutalism in concrete and steel – this building has its pipes and conduits on display. It is now badly in need of repair.

**Left:** Lasdun, Royal College of Physicians, Regent's Park, London, England, 1961-4. Designed to reflect the grandeur of Nash's neoclassical terraces nearby, this building does not imitate their eclectic style.

**Left:** Behnisch & Partners, Olympic Stadium, Munich, West Germany, 1968-72. Materials held in perfect balance – a symbol of the modern athlete.

**Below:** Ministry of Public Buildings & Works, Post Office Tower, London, England, 1962. The revolving restaurant at the top had a marvelous view.

New Brutalism was the term applied to architecture that deliberately opposed this official 'Swedish' style, and began in the works of Alison and Peter Smithson. In an attempt to find a more appropriate style for postwar Britain, the Smithsons combined austerity, structural honesty and the use of concrete in emulation of their two heroes, Mies van der Rohe and Le Corbusier. The concept of structural honesty was taken to extremes with the expression of the service elements of the building as well as materials. The first Brutalist building was their school at Hunstanton, Norfolk (1949-54), a small-scale version of Mies' buildings at IIT, interpreted with deliberate puritanism. Later Brutalist buildings abandoned the purist symmetry of the Hunstanton School in favor of an equally ruthless expression of function, replacing the steel and glass of Mies with the concrete of Le Corbusier. Le Corbusier's influence on postwar Britain was enormous. Apart from his inspiration in the development of low-cost housing, already discussed, buildings such as the Royal College of Art, London (1958-62), by Cadbury-Brown, Casson and Gooden and the Smithsons' Economist Building, London (1962-4), owe a great deal at a basic conceptual level to Le Corbusier. Maxwell Fry and Jane Drew, who collaborated with Le Corbusier in Chandigarh, disseminated Corbusian ideas through their work in

**Above:** Lasdun, University of East Anglia, Norwich, England, 1962-8. The austere and rough concrete is now being hidden by climbing ivy.

**Below:** Stirling & Gowan, Leicester University Engineering Building, England, 1959-64. Experiments with unusual forms sets this apart.

**Right:** Gibberd, Liverpool Cathedral, England, 1960-7. Leaks and other problems will cost $8,500,000 to repair.

Africa and the Middle East. Denys Lasdun's extension to the Royal College of Physicians in Regent's Park, London (1961-4), with its thin, vertical windows set irregularly along an overhanging upper story, combines elements from Le Corbusier's monastery of La Tourette.

Anticipating future educational needs, a number of new universities were founded, providing the opportunity for the design of some interesting projects, like Sussex University, Brighton (1963), which was designed by Sir Basil Spence, the architect of Coventry Cathedral (1951-63), rebuilt after the wartime blitz. The complex of buildings at York University (1962-5) by Matthew and Johnson-Marshall is centered on a man-made lake and constructed using the CLASP system of standardized prefabrication to lessen costs and speed completion. Le Corbusier's influence on Lasdun's University of East Anglia (1962-8) shows in his use of heavy concrete blocks. The complex stepped-back clusters of student residences are arranged along a spine of teaching blocks and linked by high-level walkways providing spatial variety and reducing the need for lifts. The horizontality of the complex is balanced by the tall service towers, which are emphasized in true Brutalist fashion.

James Stirling's career began in the postwar period. Two early housing projects on Ham Common, Richmond, Surrey (1955-8), and the Avenham Estate, Preston (1959), designed in partnership with James Gowan, are dominated by the use of rough brickwork. His later designs explore unusual formal relationships and the use of glass, which he thought appropriate to the lack of extremes in the British climate, with unfortunate results. The History Faculty Library, Cambridge (1964-9), combines teach-

7091 TD
969 CWA

TIERRA Y LIBERTAD
VIVA LA REVOLUCION

ing and reading facilities in a vast brick structure dominated by huge glazed areas – in particular, the sloping roof of the reading room. The unusual stepped design reflects the large public areas on the ground floor and the increasing privacy higher up. Stirling's use of stylistic quotations, from the diagonal of Constructivism and the industrial style of the Bauhaus to the ruggedness of late Le Corbusier, resulted in a highly personal style, which found its greatest expression after the general rejection of the authoritarianism of the modern movement and the development of Post-modernism in the 1970s.

### EXPERIMENTATION IN SOUTH AMERICA AND JAPAN

Latin America suffered little from the effects of the war and there was no break in the continuity of architectural development comparable with that of Europe. The adoption of the International Style as the official architecture of Brazil in the 1930s was paralleled in Mexico in the early 1940s. This was stimulated by the appearance of Le Corbusier's *Vers Une Architecture* and the visit of Hannes Meyer by invitation of the Mexican government. The ideals of the modern movement were rapidly taken up as an appropriate expression of the progressive and socialist character of the régime, influencing town-planning and the use of tower blocks for offices and housing. Again following the Brazilian pattern, an indigenous style developed, based on traditional forms and decoration. Juan O'Gorman had designed some of the earliest International Style buildings in Mexico with his houses at San Angel (1929-30), but by the 1950s he had rejected its purity in favor of a more expressive use of form. The façade of the University Library, Mexico City (1952), is highly decorated, its sculptural form and mosaics inspired by Mexican tradition. His own house at San Angel (1956) is similar to the works of Goff and Greene in the United States.

The architecture of Felix Candela shows a different approach to expressive form, but a similar rejection of the rectilinearity of the International Style. Candela, a refugee from the Spanish Civil War, arrived in Mexico in 1939, having studied architecture in Madrid and having been influenced by Torroja's structural experiments in concrete. His first major commission in Mexico was the Cosmic Ray Pavilion in the new University City (1951-3) to commemorate the discoveries made by Valarta and Le Maître. The roof of the pavilion was constructed from two very thin concrete shells, which formed hyperbolic paraboloids, the first to be built in concrete, and the economic advantages of this method gave Candela many further commissions. His exploitation of the expressive potential of concrete led to the

**Left:** O'Gorman, University Library, Mexico City, Mexico, 1952. This modern outline shows strong local influence in its use of highly colored mosaics.

**Below:** Niemeyer, Secretariat Building, Brasilia, Brazil, 1956. This is visually dramatic, but a practical failure. Those who can afford to live in Rio commute by air to this capital city – a center surrounded by slums.

angular forms of his masterpiece, the Church of the Miraculous Virgin, Mexico City (1954) and to a restaurant, Los Manantiales, Xochimilco (1958), whose eight parabolic arches give the impression of an exotic shell, enhanced by its setting in a floating garden.

The decision to build Brasilia, the new capital of Brazil, in virgin territory some 1000 miles inland from the traditional capital, Rio de Janeiro, presented a spectacular opportunity for architects. The plan for Brasilia was drawn up by Costa in 1956 and based on Le Corbusier's theories of urban development. Costa's rigid functional zoning separated industrial, residential and recreational areas, and focused the city around the government offices, designed by Niemeyer. The formal austerity of the complex, which consists of the Presidential Palace, Supreme Court and Congress buildings arranged around vast open spaces, deliberately invokes awe. In contrast to Niemeyer's earlier familiar and rounded forms, these buildings are impersonal in the extreme. The vast double slab of the Secretariat, in imitation of the UN Secretariat in New York, contrasts with the flanking saucers – concave on the Assembly, convex on the Senate. These highly simplified formal images were intended to express grandeur and monumentality, which they do, but the supremacy of form over function also successfully conveys the remoteness of government from the people, who live physically and visually apart in the huge shanty-town nearby.

Brasilia illustrates the problems involved in the rigidity of Le Corbusier's prewar theories, which had been recognized by Team X in the early 1950s. Le Corbusier's postwar works were an important influence on Affonso Reidy's Pedregulho Estate, Rio de Janeiro (1948-54), which included a school, clinic, gymnasium and swimming-pool, as well as over 270 apartments set on *pilotis*. As a rule, Latin America adopted the visual appearance of the International Style, and its connotations of a Western scale of wealth, rather than its theoretical beliefs. This has resulted in a large quantity of eclectic buildings, reflecting the aspirations of an area of the world where intense pressure for urban development is a result of rapid and unstable industrial growth.

Western influence on Japanese architecture began after the end of the isolationist Shogunate rule in 1868, and it proceeded very slowly. One of the first direct architectural contacts with the West was due to the Japanese royal family, who commissioned the Tokyo Hotel from Frank Lloyd Wright in 1915. Between the wars, the ideals and style of the modern movement began to permeate Japanese architecture through the visits of Mayekawa, Sakakura and others to Europe. The rise of nationalist militarism in the late 1930s reversed this pattern in much the same way as in Hitler's Germany, and there was a return to traditional forms and decoration, known as the Imperial Crown style. The problems of reconstruction after the war were compounded by the serious psychological effects of defeat and the complete devastation of Hiroshima and Nagasaki by atomic bombs. The competition for the Peace Center, Hiroshima (1946), was won by Kenzo Tange, a pupil of Mayekawa, and the building (1949-55), with its *pilotis*, owes much to Le Corbusier. Le Corbusier's postwar use of rough concrete was taken up by a number of Japanese architects, including Mayekawa and Tange. Mayekawa's

**Right:** Candela, Church of the Miraculous Virgin, Mexico City, Mexico, 1954. The dramatic exploitation of the potential of concrete creates an appropriate setting for the Miraculous Virgin.

**Above:** Tange, Olympic Stadium, Tokyo, Japan, 1964. An aggressive statement in steel of the power of modern technology.

Harumi apartment block, Tokyo (1957-9), is a reworking of the Unité d'Habitation, with a strong sculptural use of concrete in the splay-footed piers supporting the block. His Kyoto Town Hall (1958-60) has a heavy curved roof overhanging the building, which is reminiscent of Le Corbusier's work at Chandigarh. Tange's interpretation of the Corbusian theme in the Kagawa Prefectural Office Building, Takamatsu (1955-8), is fused with Japanese tradition.

One of the most pressing problems facing postwar architects in Japan was the shortage of usable land to house a rising population. Japanese experimentation with novel forms of housing was a direct result of this shortage and Tange's Tokyo Bay project (1959-60) was an attempt to put right the problem by creating a 'suburb' in the water. The importance of Japanese tradition to Tange is illustrated in this project, which encompassed the ideals of the Metabolist movement, comparing buildings and cities to nature and its seasonal cycles of growth and degeneration. This concept of change, essential to the Metabolists, has its roots in Japanese culture. Tange's plan was capable of being continually extended or contracted by the use of plugin units and this was taken up by the Metabolists, notably Kiyonari Kikutake in his floating Marine City project (1958), Arata Isozaki's Clusters in the Air project (1962), and Kisho Kurokawa's Nagakin Capsule Tower, Tokyo (1971). After 1960 Tange's work moved away from the basic rectangular forms of the modern movement and he explored the potential of concrete in a more original way. The Cultural Center, Nichinan (1961-3), is an exposed concrete structure of four interlocking and irregular pyramids, and his sports halls for the Tokyo Olympics (1964) experiment with elliptical plans and roofs that swing around concrete masts. Tange's development of a specifically Japanese style, that utilized the methods, details and technology of the modern Western movement but was essentially inspired by Japanese culture and philosophy, was enormously influential on the next generation of architects.

# 4/NEW FORMS: OLD THEMES

Kohn, Pedersen & Fox, 333 Wacker Drive, Chicago, Illinois, 1982-3.

**Right:** Skidmore, Owings & Merrill, Sears Tower, Chicago, Illinois, 1968-70. The efficiency of the corporation is expressed in the simple, industrially organized structure. The use of steel and glass reflects the wealth of the patron.

The twentieth century has seen remarkable changes and events. The first powered flight by the Wright brothers took place in 1903 and in 1969 man landed on the moon. Technological advance has contributed to the unprecedented rise in material living standards worldwide and led to the devastation of two world wars. The washing-machine and the nuclear bomb are both the products of the Industrial Revolution. More recently, the development of the microchip and computers has had a significant effect in many areas of life.

The political map of the world has changed dramatically with the dissolution of the old European Empires, 'spheres of influence' replacing imperial domination in Africa, Asia and the Middle East. Demand for consumer goods in the prosperous industrialized countries has encouraged economic growth elsewhere. The economic boom of the 1960s increased demand for oil and sensationally increased Arabian wealth. Japan and Germany have both emerged from the defeat of World War II as important centers of economic power.

Industrial growth in the twentieth century has seriously depleted many of the earth's natural resources and destroyed much of the world's cultural heritage in the name of progress. The principle of built-in obsolescence is rapidly being replaced by an emphasis on the conservation of animal, mineral and vegetable resources and has led to research into alternative technology. The recognition that the pre-industrial past has something to offer the modern world is part of a wider reassessment of the value of the pursuit of wealth for its own sake and a greater emphasis on the quality of life in general.

## THE FAILURE OF THE MODERN MOVEMENT

The modern movement has failed. Created in a spirit of optimism and idealism at the beginning of a new century, it was translated into the reality of the capitalist postwar world. The architects of the modern movement aimed to establish a universal style, both international and uniform. Exclusively modern, they rejected all earlier historical styles and adopted the architectural products of the Industrial Revolution, which had been the province of the engineer rather than the architect in the nineteenth century. Taut's assertion that a building that worked well was beautiful and

**Below:** Architects' Collaborative, Johns-Manville World Headquarters, Denver, Colorado, 1973-6. A dramatic contrast with its setting, this hi-tech image reflects the changing desert sky.

Chicago Loop
94 WEST
Milwaukee
90 94 EAST
Indiana

**Above:** K-Mart Center, Troy, Michigan. Grand, glossy and stylish, this center is the image of commercial success.

one that did not was ugly, shows how they rejected traditional, élitist concepts of beauty. The socialist ideal of equality replacing old class distinctions was expressed in stylistic uniformity and standardization, regardless of status or function, with the intention that this would have a positive moral effect on its users. Its adoption in the unashamedly capitalist atmosphere of postwar America as the image of freedom from oppression inevitably weakened its socialist base, but the style has undoubtedly foundered in other areas, considered essential by its originators, notably those of function and aesthetics.

The postwar rejection of many of the stylistic features of the modern movement by Le Corbusier and Aalto encouraged a more rebellious attitude in architects such as Saarinen and Stone, but the architectural scene in the United States was dominated by the Miesian International Style. Outside America criticism was easier. Concern about the authoritarian nature of the style resulted in the Team X criticism of CIAM's urban development theories and in Japan, Mayekawa's essay, 'Thoughts on Civilization in Architecture' (1965), was a clear indictment of the inability of the International Style to satisfy human requirements. The questioning of the basic tenets of the International Style coincided with the deaths of the four leading figures in twentieth-century architecture: Frank Lloyd Wright in 1959, Le Corbusier in 1965 and Mies van der Rohe and Gropius in 1969. By the 1970s criticism had become more vociferous with, for example, Brent Bolin's *The Failure of Modern Architecture* (1976), Charles Jencks' *The Language of Post-modern Architecture* (1977) and the caustic wit of Tom Wolfe's *From Bauhaus to Our House* (1981).

Industrial design was criticized for its architectural pretensions a long time before the development of the International Style. Nineteenth-century critics disapproved of its lack of appropriate forms and decoration. Until recently twentieth-century critics had been dismissed by the architectural profession on the grounds that liking or disliking the style was irrelevant, the key issue was understanding it. The innate superiority of this approach made it difficult to dent. Outside the architectural compound the style is still judged subjectively. Prince Charles' attack on the architectural profession in Britain expressed the general dislike of the International Style and made a welcome change to the apologists. We are now back to the beginning in the search for a style appropriate for the twentieth century.

The universal application of industrial imagery to all building types has become the basis for much criticism. At one level it fails to signal

**Above:** Moretti & Corning et al, Watergate Complex, Washington DC, 1972. Impersonal and powerful, it is possible to read the more sinister aspects of this complex.

the essentially different functions of various buildings. Housing, offices, educational or cultural institutions all look the same and the only clues we have of their function are to do with scale. Thus a small house is clearly not a large auditorium. Jencks has pointed out the unintentionally misleading forms of Mies van der Rohe's IIT campus, where the boiler house with its chimney looks like a church and the rectilinear chapel needed an inscription to distinguish its spiritual function from practical appearance. Early reactions to the International Style often involved direct imagery such as Saarinen's flying TWA Building, for this reason. At another level the insistence on stylistic conformity was criticized for resulting in identical, faceless and impersonal buildings, which contributed nothing to their environment. Architects such as Aalto, Utzon and Saarinen who rejected the International Style were dismissed, in Saarinen's case as willful and frivolous!

The rejection of traditional élitist concepts of beauty and their substitution by an intellectual and moral basis for aesthetic judgment has acted as an apologia for the style. In the commercial postwar world, intellectual criteria far outweigh moral ones, which have been almost forgotten. Modern architecture is seen intellectually as a pure art form, like poetry, and judged as such. The quantity of literature dealing with the relative aesthetic success of buildings is evidence of this. But we forget Taut. It is an extraordinary fact that a building whose style derives directly from the Bauhaus ideal of beauty inherent in successful functional arrangement can be judged an aesthetic victory and a practical failure.

Other art forms are able to dispense with judgments based on functional success, but architecture, unlike painting, music, or sculpture, has a basic practical purpose, physically housing the various human activities. The gulf between the architect of a building and its users has provoked the greatest censure of the International Style. The creation of Brasilia, for all its aesthetic success, has failed from a practical point of view. Anyone who can afford it commutes from Rio by air to government offices surrounded by slums, making a mockery of the concept of a capital city. Badly designed office blocks are an eyesore and no doubt have a detrimental effect on those who work there, but ultimately it is the corporations themselves who suffer, and it is their own fault. The problems with housing are different. It is a sad and ironic fact that the driving ambition of the originators of the modern movement to improve low-cost housing, and thereby the quality of working-class lives, has produced the opposite result. The list of functional failures of the International Style is long and it includes a high percentage of the low-cost housing projects built after World War II. The classic example is Yamasaki's Pruitt-Igoe housing estate, St Louis, Missouri (1952-5), which won awards for its aesthetic achievements, but had to be demolished in 1972 because of the appalling vandalism and high crime rate of its inhabitants. So much for the belief of Gropius et al that modern architecture, with its emphasis on clean lines, purity, honesty, and simplicity, would play a social and morally improving role in society !

The issue of functional success was more important in Europe, especially in Britain, where socialist and utopian visions motivated the postwar Labour Government to design a new and better society, based on the state-ownership of wealth. These visions were expressed in plans to build quality housing for the poor, financed by the state and on a scale unprecedented in modern industrial society. The perfect opportunity to test the ideals of the modern movement, and it failed. Studies of traditional working-class communities in Britain, rehoused after the war on modern high-rise estates, have unearthed considerable dissatisfaction and an increase in stress-related illnesses. One of the great tragedies of the modern movement has been its failure at a social level. As International Style tower blocks rose for the working classes, the middle classes built their individual houses in traditional styles. They could afford to, but it created a direct association between the modern and the undesirable.

Demand for houses was great and costs rose. In order to save money, quality was sacrificed and the structural standards set by the Dudley Committee in 1944 were soon abandoned, resulting in excessively thin walls, narrow corridors and small rooms in order to maintain the politically desirable production targets. Structural defects soon began to show. In 1966 a large part of Agrigento, Italy, collapsed as a result of lack of control in enforcing the building standards. In 1968 Ronan Point, a tower block in East London, fell apart after a gas explosion. Flat roofs leaked and sometimes collapsed, large glazed areas were cold in winter, expensive to heat, and too hot in the sun. Fiberglass, developed from waste products after the war as a cheap cladding material, was found to be hazardous. The result was a lot of appalling architecture for the people least capable of changing it, the working classes.

Financial considerations have been extensively blamed for the failure of the modern movement. It has been argued that 'art' was a costly element in design and could be justifiably eliminated in projects where the budget was limited, such as low-cost housing. But this is exactly what the originators of the modern movement hoped to avoid by denuding 'art' of its élitist overtones. However, in a culture dominated by money they have manifestly failed. State patronage and financial budgets have played an important part in this defeat, imposing a universal solution that reflected the artistic ideals of the architect rather than the needs of the occupier. It has been argued that an architect is a designer, not a sociologist or a welfare worker, and on this basis it is unreasonable to evaluate his buildings on the basis of the reaction of the occupier. But who else should evaluate them? The architectural magazines? The councils who commissioned them? Even Gropius recognized that the aim of low-cost housing was to improve the workers' environment, not worsen it. He may not have succeeded but that does not mean his ideal was inherently wrong.

Once the failure of the International Style had been accepted, architects began to look for other solutions appropriate for the twentieth century. Contemporary architecture remains modern but many of the visual links with the International Style have been deliberately broken. Individualism has replaced conformity and the result has been enormous stylistic variety. Despite the variety, contemporary architecture is unified by an attempt to come to terms with the failure of the modern movement. Attempts have been made to include the occupiers of low-cost housing in its design and new solutions have been found for the problem of urban development. At a stylistic level, geometrical purity, which was seen as too boring and simple, has been rejected in favor of more complicated shapes. Standardization and austerity were too impersonal and faceless, so long repetitive façades have been enriched and even prettified! (although 'pretty' is still a term of architectural abuse.) The total rejection of historical reference demanded by the International Style has been recognized as stylistically restrictive, rootless and meaningless, so historical styles have been deliberately chosen as sources for quotation and imitation. Tradition, for all its persecution, has survived.

## SURVIVAL OF TRADITION

Architectural conservation is not new, but its history follows a pattern directly related to the vicissitudes of interest in tradition. Major efforts to save classical Rome began in the Renaissance and continued intermittently with notable success in the eighteenth and nineteenth centuries. Britain took the first steps toward the protection of her architectural heritage by legislation, setting up the Royal Commission on Historic Monuments as early as 1908. Although willing in spirit, there was a marked lack of determined action in the years that followed. In 1975 this was brought to public notice in an exhibition held in London

**Right:** Larsen, Ministry of Foreign Affairs, Riyadh, Saudi Arabia, 1979-83. Tradition is an important part of Arab culture and they see no reason why it cannot be combined with innovation and wealth.

called 'The Destruction of the Country House,' which included over 1000 historic houses at least partly demolished since 1908. Industrial and economic progress has had a disastrous effect on old buildings worldwide. Medieval city streets have been widened to accommodate the automobile, or, in the case of Rome, the monumental aspirations of Mussolini. Wartime devastation has added to the toll. The city centers of Coventry, Cologne, Warsaw and Berlin, to name a few, were almost completely destroyed during World War II. Many more buildings have been razed because they had become obsolescent.

Until recently the idea of conservation had limited appeal but this has now changed. Increasingly conscious of the cultural heritage, even relatively new countries, such as the United States, have developed a determination to preserve almost any building on the grounds of age, including nineteenth-century railroad architecture and twentieth-century Art Deco. In Britain this aversion to change has resulted in an almost automatic rejection of anything new. Criticism of the ruinous effects of modernization on historic architecture is now commonplace in Europe, even to the extent of international interference where another country's heritage is threatened. Isfahan in Iran and Medina in Tunisia have both survived out of a determination on the part of the West to save historic tradition worldwide. The threat of Medina's destruction was so serious in 1970 that UNESCO and the UN Development fund intervened to finance the rescue of the city. A similar threat to Venice, whose survival was being challenged by industrial effluent from factories on the mainland, resulted in the setting up of an international appeal body, Venice in Peril. Significant contributions were made to this fund by the Americans, Germans, French and English, all of whom are keen to preserve this most watery of cities.

Mass destruction of historic city centers in the name of progress has been substantially halted. In 1968 the British government commissioned a series of reports on British cities which resulted in positive action. Donald Insall and Associates were commissioned to restore the city center of Chester, which involved refurbishment, rebuilding and the development of pedestrianized areas to limit the destructive effects of traffic and to improve the environment for popular access. Similar efforts have been made in Italy. In Rome, the Piazza Navona was closed to traffic in 1967, closely followed by traffic restrictions in the rest of old Rome. The monuments of ancient Rome are slowly being restored and cleaned with the help of grants from the EEC. Bologna, under the control of a communist council, has made a determined effort to counter the effects of land

**Left:** Quinlan Terry, Dufours Place, London, England, 1984. Britain was always reluctant to adopt the International Style, preferring her eighteenth-century glory.

**Below:** Superdome, New Orleans, Louisiana. Outer space is used to depict the superhuman image of the athlete.

**Above:** Hertzberger, Centraal Beheer Building, Apeldoorn, the Netherlands, 1974. Recognition of the impersonality of modern architecture led to this more intimate breakup of space.

speculation in order to preserve its unique historic center. In France, the restoration of the quarter of Le Marais in Paris, the old aristocratic area, has been very successful. Some of the reconstruction after the devastation of the war simply involved copies of the old buildings, notably the city center of Warsaw, which was reconstructed as closely as possible to its prewar splendor. Many German cities were rebuilt with the intention of restoring the old image, rather than radical reconstruction.

The most cogent criticism of a blanket policy of conservation is how to use an old building if its original function is now obsolete. There are endless examples of reuse, which testify to the determination of the conservationists. Old government buildings are regularly converted into art galleries, following the Italian tradition, for example the Palazzo Publico, Siena, or the Palazzo Vecchio and the Uffizi in Florence. The nineteenth-century Romanesque police station in Boston, Massachusetts, has been converted into the Institute of Contemporary Arts. The Corn Exchange in Saffron Walden, England, is now the public library. Eighteenth-century salt works at Arc-et-Senans, France, by Ledoux, were used as a refugee center during the war and have now been converted into a conference center. Early iron-frame warehouses in the London Docks have recently been converted into luxury apartments.

The extent to which traditional architecture was ignored by the modern movement is illustrated by its marked lack of coverage in architectural textbooks. There is plenty of it from the period 1930-60 in Europe, the United States and elsewhere, although it is invariably dismissed by International Stylists and sympathizers as unworthy of consideration as proper architecture. Despite the domination of the International Style and the use of modern materials, local building styles and methods continued to be used for private housing. Often criticized for poor design, these traditional houses were popular and offered security in their visual links with the past. In Britain the favored styles were mock-Tudor and neo-Georgian, both with strong nationalist overtones. In California, the same inspiration lies behind the survival of the single-story, pitched-roof ranch house and Spanish Colonial styles.

The recent renaissance of traditional and historical styles as authentic sources for modern architecture is evidence of the general reaction to the International Style. The disastrous experience of the British adoption of the modern movement for low-cost housing developments has resulted in a return to tradition. The working classes, like the middle classes, prefer the styles of the past. Since the late 1960s London councils, such as Lewisham, have been building two-story brick terraced housing with gardens and pitched roofs, in imitation of the Victorian working-class suburbs. It is ironic that it was the Nazi régime in Germany which first rejected the International Style in favor of traditional styles for low-cost housing. Countries outside the direct influence of the modern movement, notably in the Middle East and Asia, have continued to build cheaply in traditional local styles, which have evolved over the centuries to suit their climates, finances and their tastes.

The revival of interest in historicism has had an important effect on the development of Postmodern architecture, which will be discussed below. It has also encouraged some architects to copy old styles directly. The J Paul Getty Museum, Malibu, California (1970-5) is a scholarly reconstruction of a Roman villa at Herculaneum, complete with statues. British architects such as Raymond Erith and Quinlan Terry have experimented with the revival of eighteenth-century styles. Total rejection of the past is just as exclusive as insistence on his-

**Left:** Kroll, Medical Students' Center, University of Louvain, Belgium, 1970-7 (front building): new solutions for the large block and a reaction to the gleaming, smooth uniformity of the International Style.

toricism. The modern world, like its architecture, cannot entirely reject its roots. New does not always mean better, and traditional values are not necessarily antiquated. Architectural developments of the last 15 years have shown that there is a balance between modernity and tradition.

## NEW SOLUTIONS FOR URBAN DEVELOPMENT

The Team X criticism of the urban development theories of the International Style made some cogent points on the alienating effects of the functional approach to town-planning and suggested a stronger emphasis on belonging and identification. However, most of the members of Team X remained blindly attached to the stylistic ideals of the modern movement. Only one of their members, Aldo van Eyck, criticized the alienating effects of the style itself. He recognized that despite the fact that man has remained essentially the same throughout history, modern solutions to the problem of urban development have emphasized the differences of the twentieth century, rather than recognizing continuity with the past. This criticism became more widespread as the 1960s progressed and a new approach to the problem of town-planning developed.

More human concepts of complexity and diversity on a small scale replaced the intellectual and escapist ideals of efficiency and rational organization conceived on the grand scale. Architects began to recognize that the uniform solution imposed *en masse* took no account of the inevitable differences in individual needs. Hertzberger, a Dutch architect who was a joint editor of the architectural journal *Forum* with van Eyck and Bakema, developed the idea that the architect's job was to create possibilities for the individual to interpret for himself and not to impose a rational order on them regardless of individuality. An early example of this new approach to planning on a

**Right:** Kurokawa, Nagakin Capsule Tower, Tokyo, Japan, 1971. The need for new solutions to the problem of urban housing led to this block of identical cubes as an alternative to the faceless box.

**Far right:** Erskine, Byker Estate, Newcastle-upon-Tyne, England, 1968-74. This is lively and intimate, and shows a determined effort to create low-cost housing that appealed to its residents.

**Below:** Kurokawa, Nagakin Capsule Tower, Tokyo, Japan, 1971: immaculate space-saving interiors for the Japanese businessman.

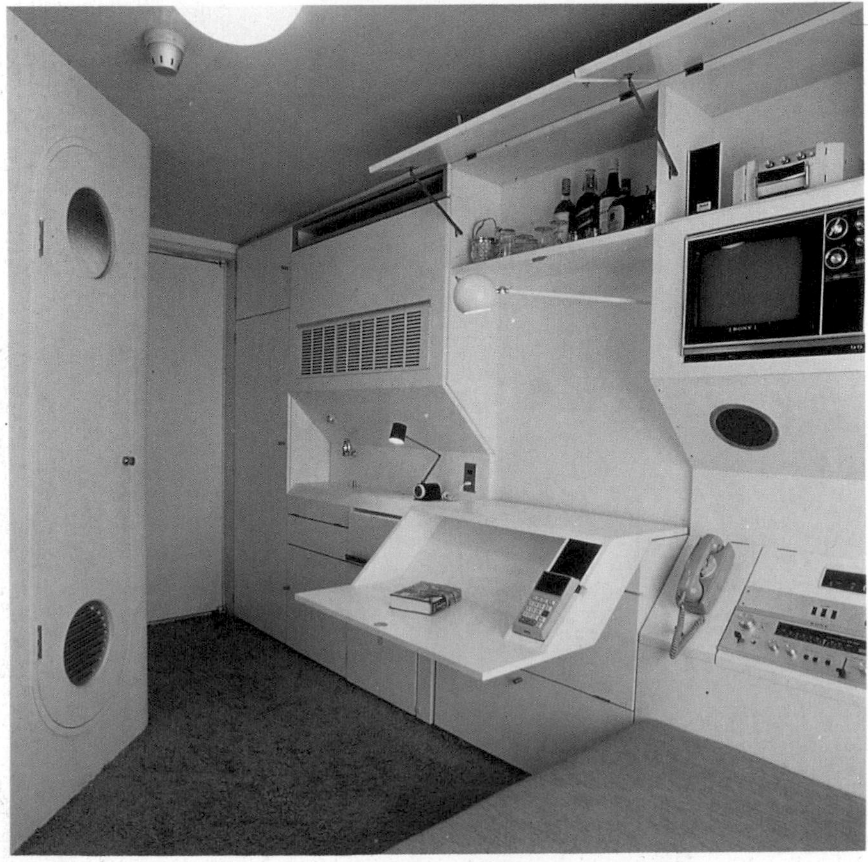

human scale was the Säynätsalo Civic Center (1949-52), designed by Aalto with changes in level and small irregular public spaces. This was followed by projects such as the competition entry by Candilis, Josic and Woods for the rebuilding of the town center of Frankfurt-Römerburg (1963). Their plan responded to the original medieval layout with a labyrinthine arrangement of buildings and public spaces, a deliberate rejection of the organizational clarity of CIAM and Le Corbusier's theories.

Breaking up the grand scale in urban development had important implications for housing. In postwar Europe the key issue for low-cost housing has been the accommodation of large numbers of people in relatively small areas. Originally the answer to the problem was seen as high-rise blocks, imitating the skyscraper as the solution for the problem of office space on small building lots. As a commercial solution it was a success, but there are other factors involved in housing and the high-rise blocks were a practical disaster. Recent developments in Britain, where the effects of the International Style in low-cost housing were particularly severe, show that high-density does not have to mean high-rise. Darbourne

Raby Crescent

**Right:** Krier, Breitenfurterstrasse, Vienna, Austria, 1987. The use of traditional features in a modern idiom reflects contemporary reaction to the International Style.

and Darke's Lillington Street estate, Pimlico, London (1966-73) is a good example of high-density housing in a variety of blocks, which are carefully arranged around small squares and center on a Victorian church. This church is built of colored brick with stone detailing and the red brick and concrete beams of the housing were deliberately chosen to unify the project. Giancarlo de Carlo's design for housing at Terni (1974-7) is also laid out with deliberate small-scale complexity, although the style of the buildings is more obviously modern. Another solution was designed by Ralph Erskine for the Byker Estate, Newcastle-upon-Tyne (1968-74). This was a traditional residential area badly in need of renewal. Instead of the

customary demolition and rehousing, the council adopted Erskine's scheme which involved partial demolition and considerably lessened the disruption for the inhabitants. The estate is bordered by two motorways and is enclosed on these sides by a long, high wall to screen off the noise and view. The façades that face the roads have a few small windows, contrasting with large balconies inside the estate. Erskine's use of different colored brick and brightly colored ventilator hoods and other features enriches, even prettifies, an otherwise daunting building, showing that architecture of the twentieth century is not necessarily faceless and impersonal.

The revival of tradition has influenced the development of a modern vernacular style. Typically it includes the use of brick and pitched roofs, with a consciously irregular arrangement of the buildings around open spaces at different levels in an attempt to re-create the village atmosphere of community life. There is also a strong regionalism about the style. Van Eyck and Theo Bosch's housing at Zwolle, the Netherlands (1975-7) follows the traditional Dutch pattern of narrow façades surmounted with gables. The steep pitch of the roofs of Feilden and Mawson's Friars Quay housing, Norwich (1972-5) continues the northern European influence on Norfolk architecture. This style deliberately combines old and new, tradition and innovation. It has been considered especially appropriate for housing and buildings whose function relates directly to ordinary, everyday life. It is very popular for shopping centers, such as the Millburngate Shopping Centre in Durham (1976) by the Building Design Partnership, and it has been commercialized as a style for roadside restaurants. At a more political level, local town halls built in the vernacular style emphasize grass roots political contact. Hillingdon Civic Centre by Robert Matthew, Johnson-Marshall and Partners (1972-7) is a series of vernacular quotations, dominated by a complex of pitched roofs all constructed in brick. It is an interesting change from the eclectic town halls of the nineteenth century, whose style derived directly from government buildings in London.

## TECHNOCRATIC IMAGES

Technological advance remains one of the most important legacies of the Industrial Revolution and the technocratic image remains the most potent image for the expression of commercial power. In response to the criticism of the uniformity of the impersonal Miesian blocks of the 1950s and 1960s the new image involves being different. The subtle formal and technical differences between the International Style business blocks were unrecognized by the architecturally illiterate public

**Above:** Pereira & Assocs, Pepperdine University, Malibu, California, 1970-5. Impersonal concrete blocks have become a popular image for education and culture.

**Right:** Johnson & Burgee, Thanksgiving Square, Dallas, Texas, 1977. Token grass is used deliberately to humanize the impersonal image of commerce.

**Below:** Roche & Dinkeloo, College Life Insurance Building, Columbus, Indiana, 1969. This is an attack on the geometric purity of the single Miesian monolith.

and they communicated nothing individual in terms of their owners nor their position. Variety now replaces similarity as the uniform for the commercial image, adding interest to the cityscape and overtly making distinctions between the companies. It is odd, in retrospect, that in office design public corporations were prepared not only to commission an image that was uniform with their rivals, but also with entirely different types of buildings. This new

uniqueness in no way detracts from the technocracy of the image – it is still as corporate and industrial now as ever – but the key issue today is one of standing out from the crowd rather than merging with it. More and more variations are designed, all with the intention of being unsubtle about their differences. This criticism of the International Style alters little apart from the visual form, leading Charles Jencks to define the stylistic variations under the heading of 'Latemodernism.'

Before the 1940s, skyscraper design had experimented with a wide variety of shapes. Some simply responded to the restrictions of the zoning laws, others to unusually shaped sites. Buildings such as the Chrysler Building adopted contemporary fashions for their decoration while others preferred the inspiration of the past, occasionally classical and often Gothic. After 1940 a few architects experimented with different forms, notably Frank Lloyd Wright's unusual hexagon plan for his Price Tower and the rounded corners to his Johnson Wax Tower. Nervi and Ponti's Pirelli Building, Gropius' Pan Am Building and the Smithsons' Economist Building all cut the corners off the cubic regularity of the Miesian box. Recent skyscraper design has developed all these ideas and added new solutions.

Attempts to break up the rectangular plan have inspired the elegant chamfering of the corners of Yamasaki's Century Plaza Towers, Los Angeles (1969-75) and his World Trade Center, New York (1962-77). This developed into a more noticeable miter on the Century Bank Building, Los Angeles (1972), by Daniel, Mann, Johnson and Mendenhall (DMJM) and their San Diego Savings and Loan Association Building, Los Angeles (1972). The sharpness of the rectangular joint between vertical skyscraper and the street is sometimes lessened by curving the lower levels of the building as it meets the ground, like SOM's Solow Building, New York (1974). Another popular way of adding interest to a rectilinear outline has been the use of the diagonal, its employment in modern architecture being justified by the Constructivists in the 1920s. Stubbins and Associates' Citycorp Center, New York (1977-8) is a white-and-silver tower of aluminum with

**Below:** Roche & Dinkeloo, One UN Plaza, New York City, 1969-76. Modern architects play games and express their individuality through a wide variety of shapes.

**Above:** Andreu et al, Charles de Gaulle Airport, Paris, France, 1974. A network of escalators organize travelers with modern efficiency.

some triangular blocks above and below. Johnson & Burgee preferred black glass for the diagonally cut twin towers of the Pennzoil Plaza, Houston (1974-5).

**Right:** Stubbins & Assocs, Citycorp Center, New York City, 1977-8. The new technocratic image: simple, impersonal but not quite a rectangular box.

**Far right:** Yamasaki, World Trade Center, New York City, 1962-77. Two towers react to the concept of a single block, but also express the growth of modern corporations.

The stepped-back style of the McGraw-Hill Building has been the inspiration for many architects, such as SOM's Sears Tower, Chicago (1968-70) or Albert C Martin and Associates' Wells Fargo Building, Los Angeles (1979). The Reunion Hotel, Dallas (1976-7) by Welton Becket Associates is stepped and clad in shimmering silver glass, which reflects the clouds. The use of reflective glass, a clever way to merge a building with its surroundings, is the ultimate means of disguising reality and creating the impersonal commercial image. Experiments with pyramidal form made by SOM in the John Hancock Center, Chicago, add visual height through perspective. Pereira's pyramid, the Transamerica Corporation building, San Francisco (1972) exploits the form for its own sake. Another variation on the theme is the suggestion of two towers in Pei's Hancock Tower, Boston (1969-75). The reality of two towers was used by Yamasaki in both the World Trade Center, New York and his Century Plaza, Los Angeles and by Johnson and Burgee for the Pennzoil Plaza, Houston.

The firm of Johnson and Burgee has taken over from Skidmore, Owings and Merrill as the creators of the new, unique commercial image. Their Post Oak Central Building, Houston (1974-6), reacts to the traditional verticality of office blocks with horizontal strips of black wrapped around the building. They have

broken up the simple Miesian block with a series of vertical steps on the IDS Center, Minneapolis (1972-5), and reinterpreted it as a pair of wedges for the Pennzoil Plaza, Houston. They have also revived traditional styles with the classically inspired 'Chippendale tallboy' of the AT & T Building, New York, complete with pediment. The even more extraordinary neo-Gothic structure for PPG Industries, Pittsburgh (1979-85) was inspired by the Victoria Tower of the Houses of Parliament in London. Their experiments with spirals have been responsible for the design of the church of Thanksgiving Square, Dallas (1977).

The reintroduction of the curve is the most complete rejection of Miesian rectilinearity. Early examples include Revell's twin curved towers for Toronto's City Hall (1958-64). A rather slicker version was designed by Kohn, Pedersen and Fox for apartments at 333 Wacker Drive, Chicago (1982-3). Circular towers have been popularized in John Portman's Regency Hyatt hotels, notably the Bonaventure Hotel, Los Angeles (1974-6). Aalto's use of a serpentine curved façade for the Baker House dormitories at MIT were finally taken up in America in the 1970s, for example DMJM's Manufacturers Bank Building, Los Angeles (1973). When used by Norman Foster, for the Willis Faber and Dumas Building, Ipswich, England (1975),it was justified as fitting in with the traditional street line.

Foster's architecture displays another aspect of the technocratic image, which derives from the Brutalist approach to an undisguised

**Above:** Johnson & Burgee, Pennzoil Plaza, Houston, Texas, 1974-5. The diagonal was given its modern status by the Constructivists at the beginning of the twentieth century.

**Far right:** Pereira, Transamerica Corporation Building, San Francisco, California, 1972. The pyramid is an inappropriate image for commerce, but its treatment here gives the right effect of originality.

**Left:** Welton Becket Assocs, Reunion Hotel, Dallas, Texas, 1976-7. An original building – the hallmark of commercial success.

**Right:** Pei, Hancock Tower, Boston, Massachusetts, 1969-75. Reflective glass invites other buildings on to a façade; for comparison or contrast?

GW

TRUMP TOWER
CHARLES JOURDAN

**Far left:** Trump Tower, New York City, 1979. This glossy and reflective façade is the ultimate in impersonal technocracy.

**Left:** Skidmore, Owings & Merrill, John Hancock Center, Chicago, Illinois, 1969. The diagonal beams emphasize the power and strength of this image, consciously different from the gloss of reflective glass.

expression of structure and services. Piano and Roger's Pompidou Center, Paris (1971-6) exaggerates this approach, coloring the structure and services and making them decorative features in their own right. Foster's Hong Kong and Shanghai Bank, Hong Kong (1979-86), is a less frivolous image, more appropriate for a bank, whose structure of piers and trusses

**Left:** Johnson & Burgee, Post Oak Central Building, Houston, Texas, 1974-6. The new and the old: a modern setback with its horizontality emphasized in the banded façade.

**Left:** Johnson & Burgee, AT & T Building, New York, 1978-82. The 'Chippendale tallboy' is easily recognizable and a good example of the recent development of traditional motifs to demodernize the commercial image.

**Right:** Johnson & Burgee, PPG Industries' Building, Pittsburgh, Pennsylvania, 1979-85. This is a dark glass version of the Houses of Parliament in England – an odd image for a modern corporation.

**Far right:** Foster, Hong Kong and Shanghai Bank, Hong Kong, 1979-86. A technological image which expresses the glamor of wealth, not the functionality of its production.

**Below:** Rogers, Lloyd's Building, London, England, 1978-86: the space-age image of technocracy with built-in service cranes on the roof picked out in blue.

forms a decorative pattern on the façade. Rogers' Lloyd's Building, London (1978-86), combines the space-age image of technocracy with references to early industrial architecture and the conservatories of Victorian England in its huge curved glass roof, which crowns the interior atrium.

Technological supremacy is still the most potent means for the expression of commercial power. There is a marked preference on the part of the corporations for an immediate, powerful and essentially visual image, that conspicuously conveys the glamor of wealth. They have no desire for a subtle, more intellectual image. After all, intellectuals are not noted for their wealth !

## BACK TO THE BEGINNING

Old themes are playing an increasingly important role in modern architecture. The growing interest in conservation and the revival of the vernacular are only part of a general trend in favor of the past. This trend has revived not only early twentieth-century forms, such as the Constructivist diagonal or the stepped-back skyscraper and Art Deco of the 1920s and 1930s, but also classical and Gothic features, notably in Johnson and Burgee's historical quotations on their skyscrapers. Other architects have gone further, developing a more meaningful, intellectual use of historical imagery, which should not be seen as quotation, nor as revivalism but as a synthesis that combines modernity and tradition.

HILTON

**Left:** Kurokawa, Sony Tower, Tokyo, 1975. The glamor of technology reflects Japanese pride in their economic success.

**Right:** Meier, Douglas House, Harbor Springs, Michigan, 1971-3. The New York Five experimented with early modern themes in their architecture, designing pure, white and geometric buildings.

Some architects have revived the purism and abstraction of the early modern movement, criticizing what they saw as the deterioration of the International Style after World War II. This approach has been dominated by the work of the New York Five – Peter Eisenman, Michael Graves, Charles Gwathmey, John Hejduk and Richard Meier – named from the book, *Five Architects* (1972), published after an exhibition of their work at the Museum of Modern Art, New York (1969). Their buildings are predominantly white and their architecture derives from early Le Corbusier, Constructivism and De Stijl, experimenting with themes such as planar interpenetration, the diagonal and spatial abstraction. Eisenman's single-minded pursuit of abstraction excluded the functionalism of early modern architects to the

**Far left:** Foster, Hong Kong and Shanghai Bank, Hong Kong, 1979-86. The overt power of modern materials is used to influence our interpretation of this corporate image.

**Left:** Johnson & Burgee, Public Library Extension, Boston, Massachusetts, 1973. Massive and inspired by classical Roman architecture; a comparison with their PPG building shows how versatile an architect now needs to be, another reference to nineteenth-century eclecticism.

**Above:** Eisenman, House VI for the Franks, Washington, Connecticut, 1972: intellectual and abstract, even in its title.

extent of building an unclimbable staircase to a nonexistent floor in House VI (for the Franks, Washington, Connecticut, 1972).

The essentially modern forms of the neo-Rationalists in Europe are based on classical and vernacular styles. The movement was launched by Aldo Rossi and others in *Architettura Razionale*, published in 1973. Rossi's architecture is based on a rational approach to design and his stripped version of classicism, typified by the Roman severity of the Modena cemetery (1973-6), is often likened to the architecture of Fascism. Rossi strongly denies this criticism, insisting on inspiration from the vernacular architecture of the Lombard plain. Rationalist sympathizers include Mario Botta, Leon and Rob Krier, J P Kleinhues, O M Ungers and Ricardo Bofill, who borrows from a wide range of styles, producing a sculptural monumentality in contrast to Rossi's linear severity.

Kahn's classical inspiration has been developed into a more overt use of classical forms by architects like Robert Venturi. Venturi, who had been a pupil of Kahn, began practicing as an architect in the late 1950s. His early buildings, notably the house for his mother, the Vanna Venturi House, Chestnut Hill, Pennsylvania (1962-4), expressed his dislike of the purist forms of then-current American architecture and its inability to communicate. His innovatory ideas on architecture have been published as *Complexity and Contradiction in Architecture* (1966) and *Learning from Las Vegas* (1972). In contrast to the simplistic images of the International Style, Venturi's designs aim to create ambiguity and a variety of levels of meaning. His buildings are not reviv-

**Left:** Venturi & Rauch, House for Mrs Venturi, Chestnut Hill, Pennsylvania, 1962-4. The pediment on the façade makes a deliberate historical reference, in contrast to the antitraditionalism of the International Style.

**Below left:** Bofill & Partners, Xanadu, Calpe, Spain, 1967. Modern and nonconformist, Bofill quotes from a wide range of styles, but the composition is modern.

alist, but they utilize historical elements that are interpreted in a modern context (some would say they are unreasonably exaggerated and distorted), such as the pediment on the Venturi House, the pitched roof of the Tucker House, Katonah, New York (1975), or the Ionic column in the Allen Art Museum, Oberlin College, Ohio (1973-7). They also make deliberate references to contemporary American pop culture. Venturi's use of conventional and therefore recognizable architectural elements communicate in the language of tradition and

**Below:** Venturi & Rauch, Guild House, Philadelphia, Pennsylvania, 1962-6. Venturi aimed to create ambiguity, in contrast to the purity of the International Style.

**Above:** Venturi, Rauch & Scott Brown, Fire Station No 4, Columbus, Indiana, 1965-7.

**Below:** Venturi, Rauch & Scott Brown, Faculty Club, Penn State University, Philadelphia, Pennsylvania, 1974-6.

mark a return to the premodern concept of decorum. He has been praised for enriching the language of architecture and criticized for returning to the despised eclecticism of the nineteenth century. He certainly quotes from past masters, including Palladio and Le Corbusier, and it is a matter of personal opinion whether this constitutes progress or retrogression. Venturi's use of multiple historical references in his buildings adds to their complexity, enabling a superficial appreciation that is often misleading and is contradicted by deeper

levels of meaning which cannot be readily understood.

Venturi's work has been a formative influence on the development of a number of architects, notably Charles Moore and Robert Stern, whose work contrasts with the deliberate abstraction of the New York Five. The battle between the Whites and the Greys (Venturi et al) resulted in Graves' increasing historicism and his decampment in favor of the Greys. Graves developed away from neomodernism toward a more historical approach. His earlier

**Above:** Venturi, Rauch & Scott Brown, Tucker House, Katonah, New York, 1975. Venturi has been praised for enriching the language of architecture and criticized for his return to eclecticism.

**Left:** Venturi, Rauch & Scott Brown, Institute for Scientific Information HQ, Philadelphia, Pennsylvania, 1978. Superficially an abstract pattern based on flower forms, but there are deeper levels of meaning less easily understood.

**Above:** Graves, Benacerraf House extension, Princeton, New Jersey, 1969. Graves' early work experimented with abstraction and interplanar penetration, inspired by the purity of the early modern movement.

**Left:** Graves, Portland Public Services Building, Portland, Oregon, 1981-3. In contrast to his early 'white' style, Graves then developed the use of color, retaining abstract forms.

**Right:** Graves, Humana Medical Corporation HQ, Louisville, Kentucky, 1982-7: the postmodern image for the discerning corporation.

preference for white has been replaced by more colorful buildings, but these retain the highly abstracted interpretation of his former style. Moore's architecture relates to the revival of more public elements of classical imagery than Venturi, for example his 'rural acropolis' of the Kresge College complex, University of California at Santa Cruz (1973-4), or the urban context of his Piazza d'Italia in New Orleans (1975-8). Other architects who have experimented with the development of the language of architecture include Frank Gehry, Stanley Tigerman and SITE Inc & James Wines.

Venturi, Graves, Moore and Stern are the key figures in Charles Jencks' exclusive concept of Postmodernism. As yet there is confusion in the exact definition of the term. Charles Jencks, who popularized its use, defines it as multivalent, using the language of architecture to communicate on both popular and élitist levels, in contrast to the univalence of the International Style. Other writers have generalized the concept of Postmodernism and included any deviation from the International Style under its umbrella. Jencks makes a clear distinction between Latemodernism, the exagger-

**Above:** Venturi, Rauch & Scott Brown, Gordon WU Hall, Butler College, Princeton, New Jersey, 1983. Classical quotations include the thermal window and semicircular apse, balanced with steel-frame windows.

**Left:** Gwathmey, East Campus Complex, Columbia University, New York, 1981: the postmodern image for the intellectual institution.

**Right:** Moore, Burns House, Los Angeles, California, 1974. The swimming pool is part of the image.

**Far right:** Isozaki, Tsukuba Civic Center, Japan, 1980-3. The architecture has been smoothed out of the roughness of nature.

**Below:** SITE Inc & James Wines, Best Products Retail Store, 'Notch' showroom, Sacramento, California, 1977. Architecture can be fun again.

ation of essentially modern forms, and Postmodernism, a new language and ideology. The International Style was criticized for being too conceptual and remote, architecture for architects and not for people. At a purely visual level, both Latemodernists and Postmodernists have done much to change this. However, at an ideological level architects, especially the Postmodernists, have developed the intellectual status of architecture to a level far removed from popular comprehension, shrouding it in linguistic mysticism and Structuralist theory.

**Right:** Isozaki, Fujimi Country Clubhouse, Oita, Japan, 1972-4. The classically inspired portico indicates that this is a place of status.

Jencks' concept of multivalence is an expression of this, the higher or deeper levels of meaning within a Postmodernist building being comprehensible only to an élite and the 'real meaning' being still obscure.

A marked distinction exists between the commercial élitism of the Latemodernists and the intellectual élitism of Postmodern architecture, cloaked in its popular imagery. One of the most radical aims of the founders of the modern movement was to rid architecture of its élitism. They rejected the traditional nineteenth-century distinction between Building and Architecture, considering industrial structures and workers' housing just as much part of architecture as churches and museums. Hitchcock and Johnson's catalogue for the 1932 International Style exhibition included commercial and industrial buildings as well as state and private commissions. The criteria for consideration were stylistic, and buildings were rejected for their lack of conformity to the new rules, not for any intrinsic difference of type. Jencks' distinction between Latemodernism and Postmodernism suggests that we have returned to the intellectual snobbery and élitism of the nineteenth century.

## IMAGES FOR CULTURE?

If any further proof is needed of the current interest in the past, it is in the recent spate of

**Right:** Foster, Sainsbury Centre for the Visual Arts, Norwich, England, 1977. Technology as an image of culture? The aluminum skin is leaking and will soon be replaced with white boards.

museum and art-gallery building. The collecting of works of art is a strong reaffirmation of the classical tradition, and has been since the Renaissance. The modern movement was ambivalent in its attitude to the museum, a building that represented not only the culture of the past they had rejected, but also bourgeois wealth. The International Style was entirely inappropriate for the design of museums and it is not surprising that relatively few were built. The bewildering variety of current stylistic trends is reflected in the vast range of styles used for recent museums and art galleries. Unlike commercial architecture, which is dominated by the technocratic image, the architecture of culture is highly diverse and reflects the current trend toward individualism. It also displays the growing awareness of the possibilities of an architectural language for communication.

The technocratic image is used almost frivolously in Piano and Rogers' Centre Pompidou, Paris (1971-6). The message that art is fun is directed at youth, not age. In contrast, Foster's Sainsbury Centre, Norwich (1977) emphasizes the glamor of a private and personal collection funded by commercial wealth (somewhat inappropriate for the Art History Department of the University of East Anglia which is also housed in the building). The breakdown of the rectangular and open spaces of the International Style in favor of more humanized, small-scale development for museums was pursued by architects such as Aldo van Eyck in his Arnhem Pavilion (1966), and the little intimate museum has proved particularly popular for the display of everyday life in small towns throughout Europe and the United States.

**Above:** Pei, National Gallery of Art, East Building, Washington DC, 1978: the impersonal image for culture.

**Below:** Piano & Rogers, Centre Pompidou, Paris, France, 1971-6. This shows that art can be fun – a message for youth.

**Right:** Pei, Everson Museum, Syracuse, New York, 1968. The museum requires a special sort of courage to enter.

**Below:** Johnson & Burgee, Art Museum of South Texas, Corpus Christi, Texas, 1972. The bleak, concrete image gives us no clues about what we will find inside.

These intimate museums contrast strongly with the impersonal concrete blocks of Pei's East Building for the National Gallery, Washington DC (1978), his Everson Museum, Syracuse, New York (1968), or Johnson and Burgee's Art Museum of South Texas, Corpus Christi, Texas (1972), all of which derive from Kahn's concrete wall for his extension to the neoclassical Art Gallery at Yale. This bleak and unwelcoming image for culture is remarkably

**Left:** Meier, High Museum of Art, Atlanta, Georgia, 1980-3. Recent revivalism includes the early modern movement among its options.

popular. It expresses contemporary attitudes to culture, such as the difficulty of initiation into this new and exciting world, or its distance from everyday life, and it acts as a challenge to the mental aerobics of art appreciation.

The role of tradition follows the pattern of more general architectural developments, straight revivalism and modern interpretations of older styles. Moneo's Museo de Arte Romano, Merida, Spain (1981-5), revives

**Below:** Neuerburg et al, Getty Museum, Malibu, California, 1970-5. Reviving an image of private wealth of the past is entirely appropriate.

**Right:** Stirling, Staatsgalerie extension, Stuttgart, West Germany, 1977-84. A series of modern quotations from Le Corbusier to Aalto, set on marble-faced classical solidity.

Roman architecture both in terms of scale and its brick arch construction. The exhibits themselves are the remains of Roman civilization in Spain and this is cleverly suggested in the exposed brickwork, 'ruined' by the implied removal of its original marble facing. This image of the fall of the Roman Empire contrasts strongly with the J Paul Getty Museum, Malibu (1970-5), which unquestionably revives the power, wealth and grand tastes of the Roman Empire. This image of the private wealth of the past is entirely appropriate for the Getty fortune and for what is probably the only museum in the world that can compete with the scale and quality of art collections of the past.

Venturi and Rauch's addition to the Allen Art Museum, Oberlin College, Ohio (1973-7), is a much wittier interpretation of classical culture, with its use of the oversized Ionic column emphasizing the intellectual legacy of Greece, rather than the imperial legacy of Rome. Post-modernism is an entirely appropriate style for expressing the ambiguity of the monetary and intellectual contexts of culture. Stirling's Staatsgalerie extension, Stuttgart (1977-84) involves a series of modern quotations, which range from Corbusian strip windows and De

**Above:** Venturi, Rauch & Scott Brown, Allen Art Museum, Oberlin College, Ohio, 1973-7. Their extension on the right uses the same colors as the main block, but the contrast is still extreme.

**Left:** Stirling, Staatsgalerie extension, Stuttgart, West Germany, 1977-84. Coloring detail revives De Stijl, but Stirling does not restrict himself to their insistence on red, yellow and blue.

**Right:** Ungers, Badisches Landesbibliothek, Karlsruhe, West Germany, 1979-85. Tradition has survived the onslaught of the modern movement.

**Below:** Stirling, Tate Gallery, Clore extension, London, England, 1987. Architecturally invigorating but the beige interior manages to provide a totally inadequate showroom for Turner's art.

**Left:** Hollein, Städtisches Museum, Abteiburg, Mönchengladbach, West Germany, 1972-82. An attempt to break up the monolithic image and re-create a village atmosphere within the context of modern style.

Stijl colored details (although not restricted to primary colors) to a huge serpentine window, reminiscent of Aalto's Finnish Pavilion for the New York World's Fair (1939). These thin, metal quotations sit with deliberate discomfort on solid structure, whose marble facings and simple geometrical forms refer to classical tradition.

The variety of current stylistic trends is bewildering. Individualism dominates in marked contrast to the uniformity of the International Style. In 1914 the battle between the individualists and the conformists resulted in victory for Gropius and Muthesius and the superiority of the machine aesthetic, standardization, conformity and modernity. In recent years we have returned to the same position, but this time the conflict appears to favor van der Velde's insistence on individualism, creativity and traditionalism. Attempts to categorize current architectural trends, a natural preliminary to understanding, have been complicated by a determination on the part of intellectually élitist architects to retain the mystique in which their creativity is shrouded. Many architects refuse to be categorized. One important legacy of the Bauhaus has been the intellectualization of the process and reasoning of architectural creativity. The intellectual context of a building is by no means always discernible from its form and decoration and this has led Charles Jencks to define the difference between a single level of interpretation and a number of levels in terms of 'univalence' and 'multivalence' in architecture. The implication that multivalence, the determining factor of Postmodernism, is superior to univalence, or Late-modernism, carefully retains all the intellectual élitism of the International Style, both styles being equal in their options for mass appeal.

It is difficult to be conclusive about the variety of trends in contemporary architecture. The excitement and idealism that accompanied the birth of the modern movement has dissolved in a difficult adolescence, in much the same way as the Renaissance developed (some would say, deteriorated) into Mannerism. The International Style may be dead, but life goes on and so does architecture.

# INDEX

Page numbers in *italics* refer to illustrations.

# ACKNOWLEDGMENTS

The publisher would like to thank Tanya Hines the editor, Martin Bristow the designer, Mandy Little and Moira Dykes the picture researchers and Ron Watson who prepared the index. We would also like to thank the following picture agencies, institutions and individuals for supplying the illustrations as listed below:
**Peter Aaron/ESTO:** 42, 43. **Wayne Andrews/ESTO:** 12(bottom), 15(bottom), 17, 26(bottom), 52, 69. **Architects' Collaborative** (© Nick Wheeler Photographics): 148. **Architectural Association, London Slide Library:** 15(top), 23(top), 24, 26(top), 27, 30(both), 35, 39, 78, 82(top), 83(top), 87(top), 90(top left), 97, 110, 118(bottom), 127, 135(both), 142, 144, 154, 174(bottom), 178(bottom left), 180(top), 187(bottom). **Architectural Press:** 99(top); Reinhard Friedrich 121, 189. **Art Institute of Chicago:** 10. **James Austin:** 111(top), 183(bottom). **C. H. Bastin & J. Evrard:** 21. **BBC Hulton Picture Library:** 8, 12(top), 76(bottom). **BBC Hulton/Bettmann Archive:** 13, 16(both). **Alan & Sylvia Blanc F/ARIBA:** 58(bottom), 59, 65(top), 90(top left), 98(top), 108(bottom), 111(bottom), 126(bottom), 134(bottom). **Brazilian Embassy:** 143. **The British Architectural Library, RIBA, London:** 33(top), 34, 37, 38, 49, 54, 59(top), 81, 133. **Richard Bryant/ARCAID:** 19(top & bottom), 55, 75(top), 91, 113(bottom), 129, 138-9, 153, 172, 175(both), 186(bottom). **G. Candilis:** 126(top). **Martin Charles:** 4, 6, 63, 65(bottom), 66(top), 123(top), 170(bottom). **Conway Library/Courtauld Institute:** 20, 29(bottom), 33(bottom), 36(top), 57(bottom), 59(top), 112. **Joseph Coughlan:** 139. **Coventry Cathedral:** 136. **The Design Museum:** 44. **Charles Eames:** 109(top). **R. Einzig/ARCAID:** 140(bottom). **Eisenman Robertson:** 174(top). **Foster Associates** (Ian Lambot): 171. **Foundation le Corbusier:** 64, 109(bottom). **J. Paul Getty Museum** (Julius Shulman): 185(bottom). **Michael Graves** (Paschall/Taylor): 178(bottom right), 179(top). **Greater London Photograph Library:** 25, 70(bottom). **Gwathmey Siegel & Assocs** (Richard Payne AIA): 179(bottom). **Herman Hertzberger:** 156. **Angelo Hornak:** 22(both), 23(bottom), 31(both), 50, 51, 67(bottom), 71(bottom), 74(top), 94, 99(bottom), 103(both), 115, 164(top). **Hyatt Regency Hotels:** 166(bottom left). **Wolfgang Hoyt/ESTO:** 168. **Arata Isozaki** (Yasuhiro Ishimoto): 181, 182(top). **Japan Information Centre:** 145(top). **Johnson/Burgee Architects:** 108(top), 170(top right); Richard Payne AIA: 106(bottom), 166(top), 169(bottom), 173(bottom), 184(bottom); Timothy Hursley: 170(top left). **Johnson Wax Company:** 92, 133(top). **Keystone Collection:** 28, 53(top), 72, 75(bottom), 105(bottom), 141, 165. **Kimbell Art Museum:** 124. **Kisho Kurokawa Architects** (Tomio Ohashi): 158(both), 173(top left). **Kohn, Pedersen & Fox:** 146. **Rob Krier:** 160. **Lucien Kroll:** 157. **Denys Lasdun, Peter Softley & Assocs:** 137(bottom), 140(top). **Dieter Leistner:** 188(top). **John Margolies/ESTO:** 73. **Peter Mauss/ESTO:** 14. **MARS:** 68, 83(bottom), 119(top)/Bundesarchiv Koblenz 79(bottom), 80(bottom), /CEGB 70(top), /Foster Assocs 182(bottom), /Johnson Wax Company 90(bottom), /K-Mart 150, /J. E. Seagram 101, /UN 77(top). **Moore, Rubel & Yudell** (John Nicolai): 180(top). **Michael Moran:** 7. **Museum of Finnish Architecture:** 85, 88, 131, 132. **Museum of Modern Art:** 41, 60, 61(both), 62, 80(top). **Nederlands Documentatiecentrum voor de Bouwkurist:** 53(bottom). **Novosti Press Agency:** 77, 79(top). **Osterreichische Nationalbibliothek:** 29(top), 32(top). **Pacific Design Center** (Martin Rand): 1. **I. M. Pei & Partners** (Ezra Stoller/ ESTO]: 184(top). **Pepperdine University:** 161. **Pereira & Assocs:** 167. **Photosource:** 2, 46, 71(top), 104, 107, 159. **Kevin Roche, John Dinkeloo & Assocs:** 162(bottom), 163. **Rheinisches Bildarchiv:** 40, 45. **The Salk Institute:** 122(bottom). **Alison & Peter Smithson:** 137(top). **James Stirling, Michael Wilford & Associates** (Richard Bryant): 188. **Ezra Stoller/ESTO:** 90, 93, 102, 104, 105(top), 116(both), 117(both), 149, 169(top), 173(top right), 185(top). **Swiss National Tourist Office:** 36. **Venturi, Rauch & Scott Brown** Tom Bernard: 176(both), 177(bottom), 178(top), 186-7, Tom Crane: 177. **Weidenfeld Archive/ Bildarchiv Foto Marburg:** 56 Hendrich Blessing: 100 John Donat: 120(top). **Stuart Windsor:** 66(bottom), 74(bottom), 98(bottom), 114(both), 119(bottom), 134(top), 151, 155, 162(top), 164(bottom), 166(bottom right), 183(top). **Frank Lloyd Wright Foundation:** 18(both). **Yale Center for British Art** (Tom Brown): 125. **Yale University:** 118(top). **Jack Zehrt:** 11. **Zoological Society of London:** 86.